Studies in Geometry Series

Triangles

Workbook

Calculating Measurements and Ratios

Tammy Pelli

D1507429

© 2004 by Stanley H. Collins
All rights strictly reserved.

Published by:
Garlic Press
605 Powers St.
Eugene, OR 97402

ISBN 1-930820-44-5
Order Number GP-144

www.garlicpress.com

Table of Contents

Introduction

About This Workbook

- There are many topics in geometry which involve triangles. The purpose of this workbook is to explore some of those ideas. The fundamentals of geometry are required to develop the specific applications to triangles. Reminders of the basics are given, as needed, in the text, but the student does need to be familiar with the basics of lines, segments, angles, etc.

- Because every textbook is different, reference to specific theorems and postulates is not made overtly so that this workbook can complement a student's study of geometry without conflicting with his/her schoolwork. Many theorems, postulates and definitions are presented informally and their applications are developed in the explanation and the practice exercises.

- This book requires basic algebra skills. Algebra is used as a method of explanation for some of the ideas presented. Additionally, algebraic examples are integrated into the practice exercises.

- This book requires some familiarity with radicals. Some problems involve simplifying and multiplying radicals.

- Towards the end of the workbook, you will find an Exam so that you can check to find if you have mastered the concepts presented here.

- A brief Glossary of vocabulary and basic concepts is found at the end of the workbook, before the Answer Key.

- The Answer Key provides the answers to all practice exercises. In many cases, it also provides a thorough explanation of the thinking involved in the problem.

Chapter 1

Triangle Basics

What Is a Triangle?

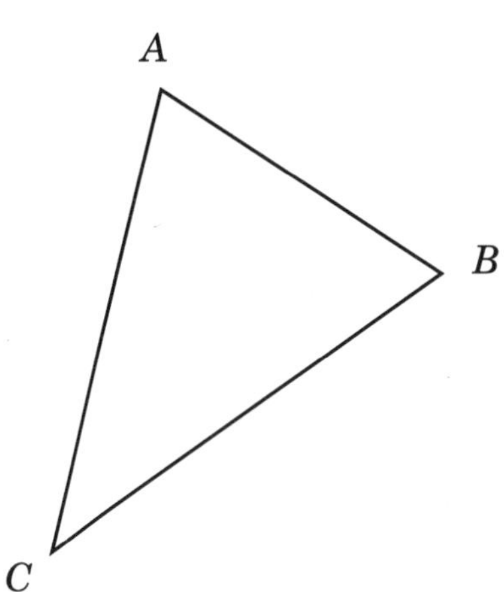

- ***A triangle has 3 sides which meet in three vertices.***
  Sides: $\overline{AB}$, $\overline{BC}$, $\overline{CA}$. These are read as "segment *AB*" or "side *AB*."
  Vertices (singular = vertex): *A*, *B*, *C*. These are read as "*A*" or "vertex *A*."

- ***The angles of a triangle always add up to 180º.***
  Angles: $\angle A$ (or $\angle CAB$, or $\angle BAC$), $\angle B$ and $\angle C$.
  These are read "angle *A*" or "angle *CAB*."
  - If you want to refer to the measure of the angle, and not its name, use the notation: $m\angle A$. This is read "the measure of angle *A*."

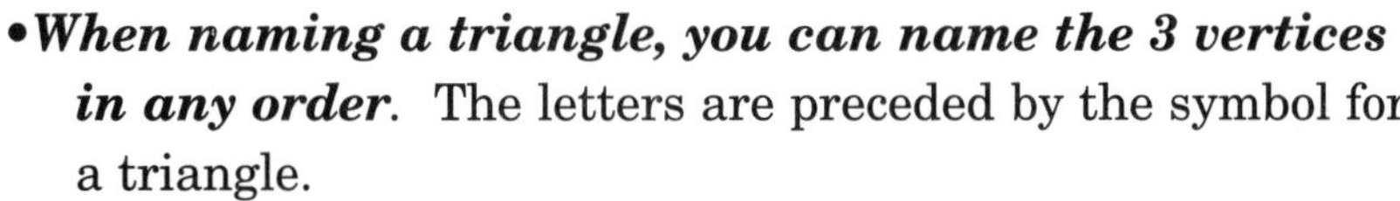

- ***When naming a triangle, you can name the 3 vertices in any order***. The letters are preceded by the symbol for a triangle.
  Names for this triangle: ΔABC, ΔBAC, ΔCAB, ΔACB, ΔBCA, ΔCBA.
  These are read as "triangle *ABC*."

Practice

Name these triangles and name each of their angles.

Example

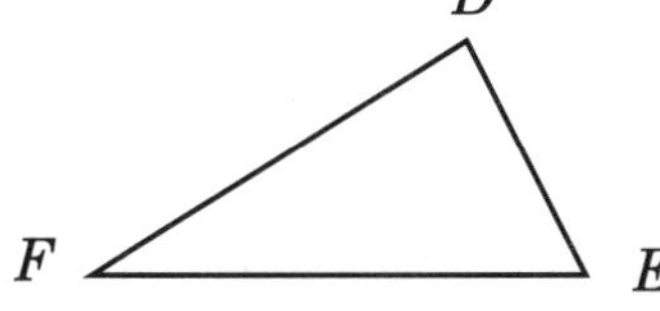

Options for naming the triangle above include:
ΔDEF, ΔFED and ΔEDF, among others. Options for naming the angles include: $\angle D$, $\angle F$ and $\angle E$ or $\angle EDF$, $\angle EFD$ and $\angle$DEF.

1.

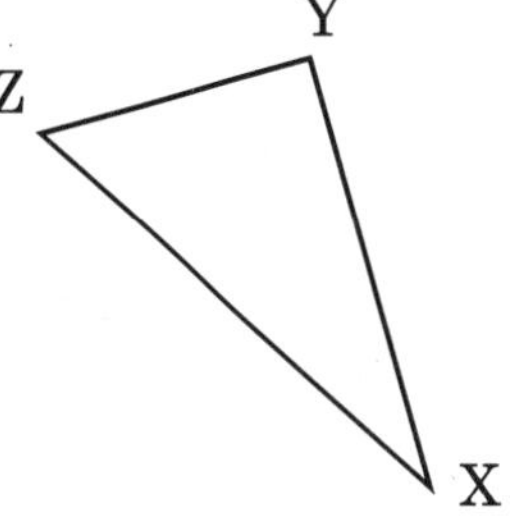

2. **3.**

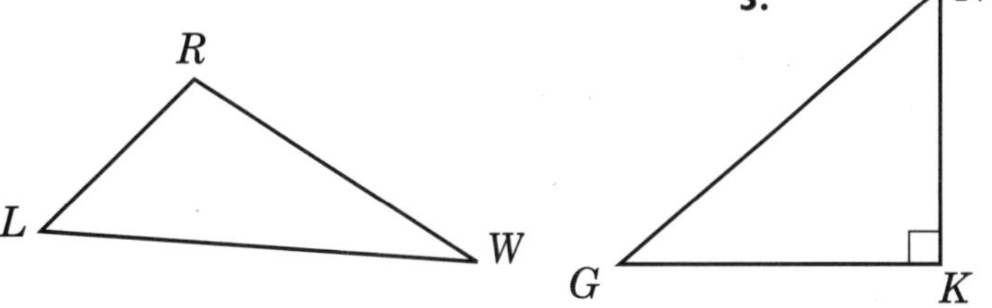

4.

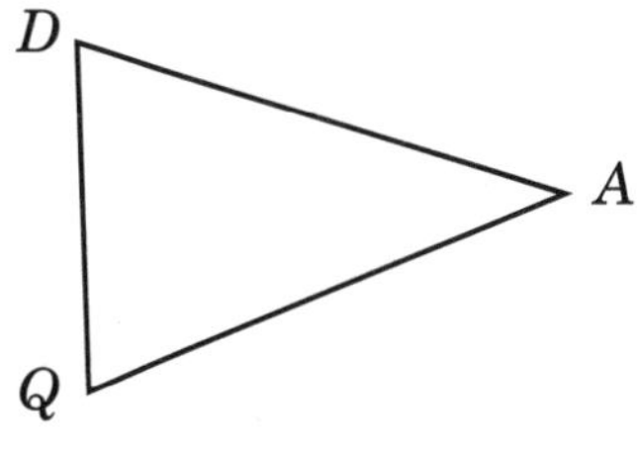

Types of Triangles

Triangles can be classified by two characteristics: angles and sides.

Focus on Angles

A. ***Acute Triangle:*** a triangle with 3 acute angles

- Acute angles measure 0° – 90°.

B. ***Right Triangle:*** a triangle with 1 right angle and 2 complementary acute angles.

- Right angles measure 90°.
- Complementary angles are a pair of angles with a sum of 90°.

C. ***Obtuse Triangle:*** a triangle with 1 obtuse angle and 2 acute angles.

- Obtuse angles measure 90° – 180°.

D. ***Equiangular Triangle:*** a triangle with 3 congruent angles.

- Congruent angles have the same measure.
- Each angle will measure 60°.

Focus on Sides

E. ***Scalene Triangle:*** a triangle in which all sides have different lengths.

F. ***Isosceles Triangle:*** a triangle with at least 2 congruent sides and 2 congruent angles.

G. ***Equilateral Triangle:*** a triangle with 3 congruent sides.

- All equilateral triangles are also equiangular triangles (3 congruent sides and 3 congruent angles).
- All equilateral triangles are also isosceles triangles because they have at least 2 congruent sides.

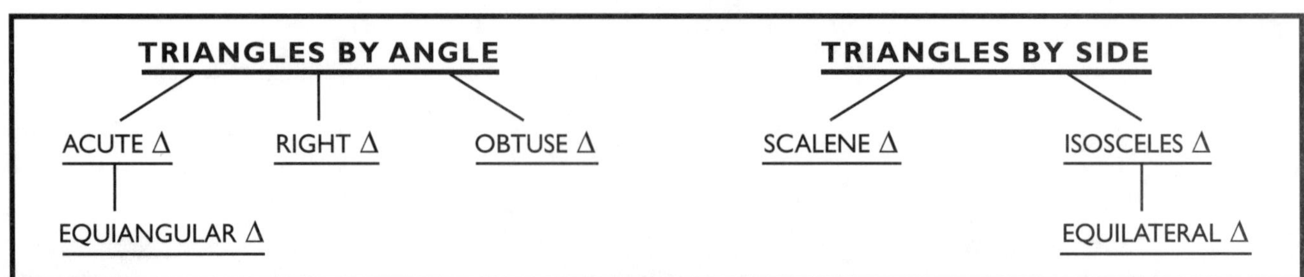

Combining Classifications

To fully describe a triangle, you need a name which describes both the sides and the angles. But not all angle classifications can be paired with all side classifications.

Acute Triangle Possibilities

Acute Scalene

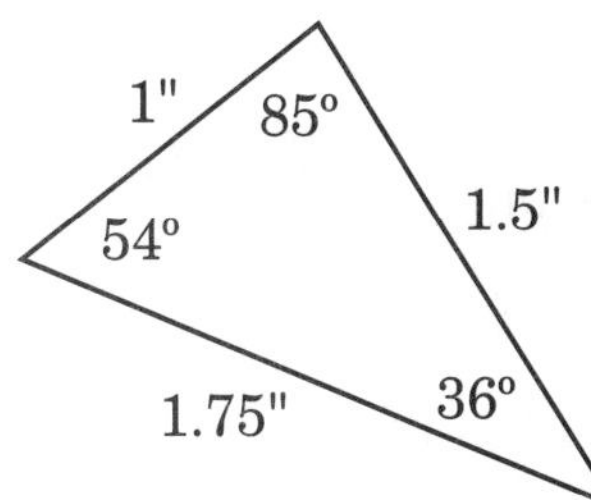

Acute Isosceles

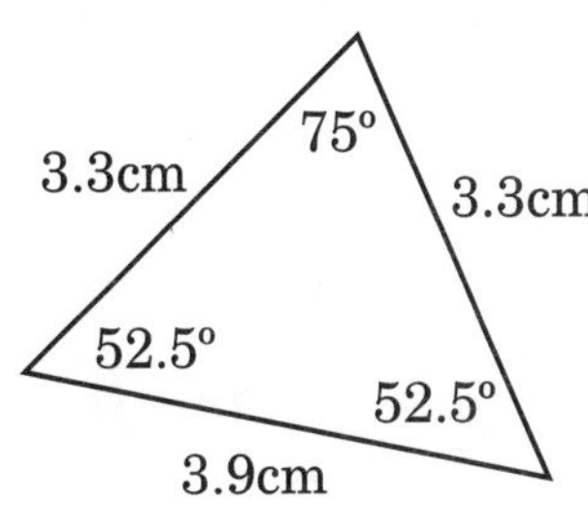

Equiangular / Equilateral

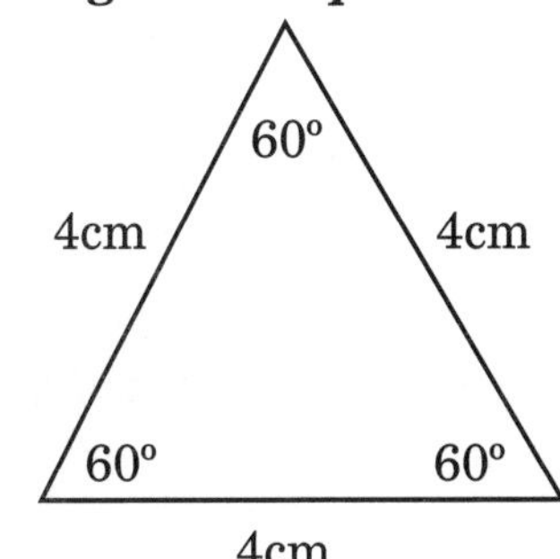

Obtuse Triangle Possibilities

Obtuse Scalene

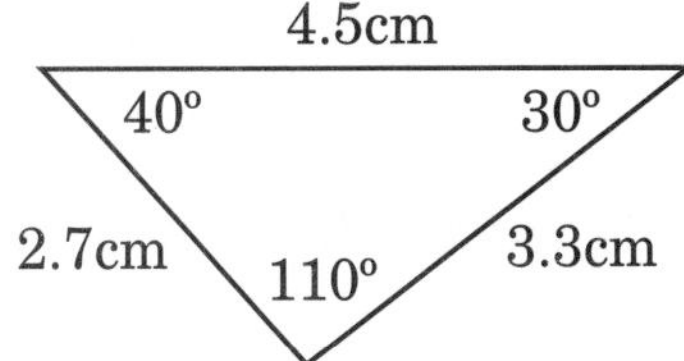

Obtuse Isosceles

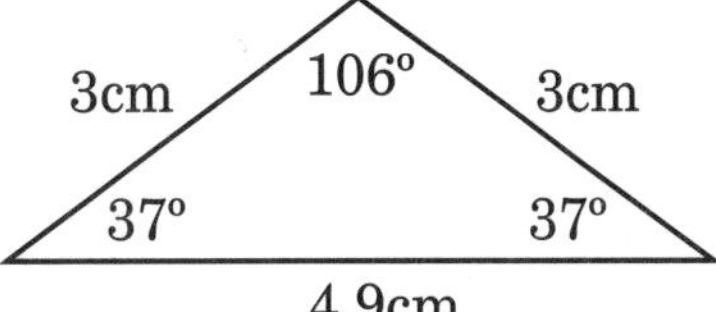

Right Triangle Possibilities

Right Scalene

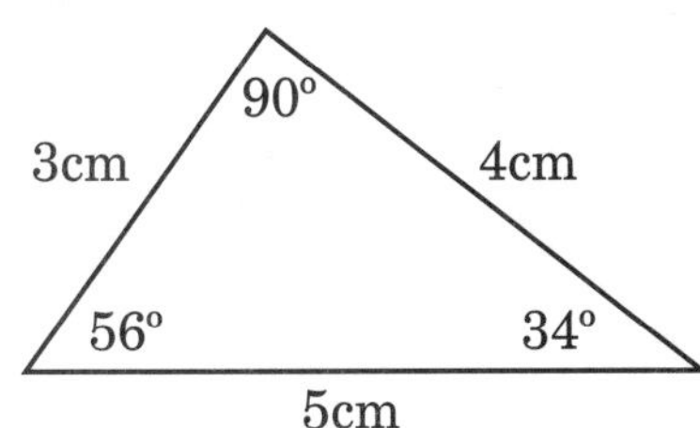

Right Isosceles

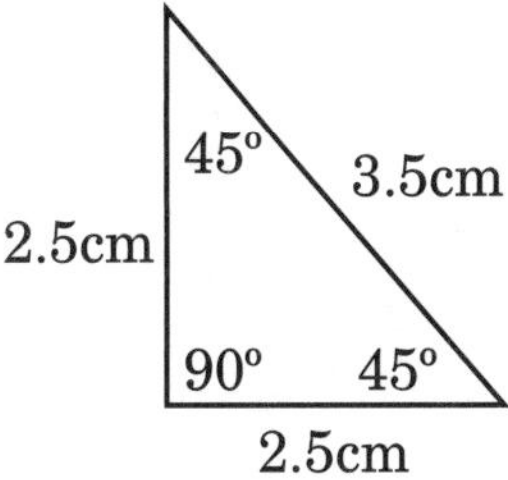

Practice

Use a ruler and a protractor to measure the sides and angles. Then determine the type of triangle.

1.

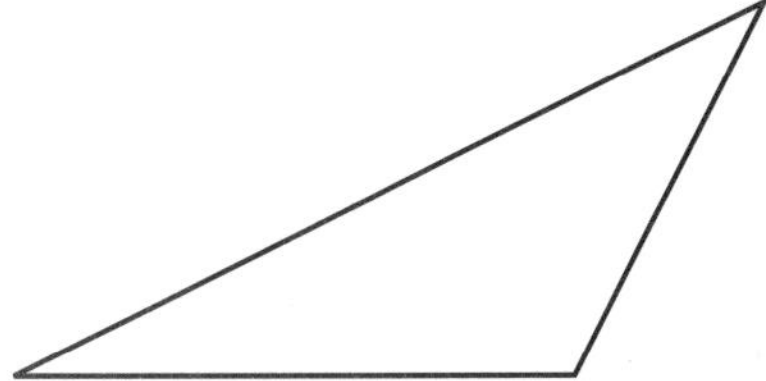

2.

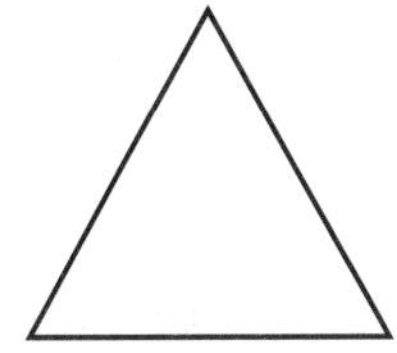
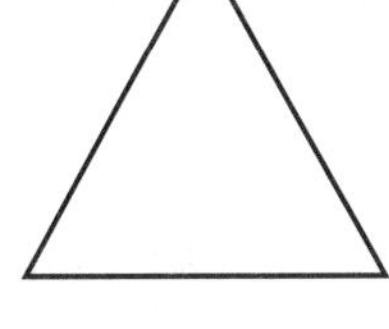

3.

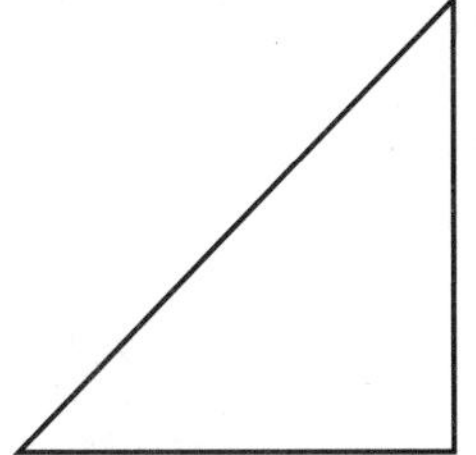
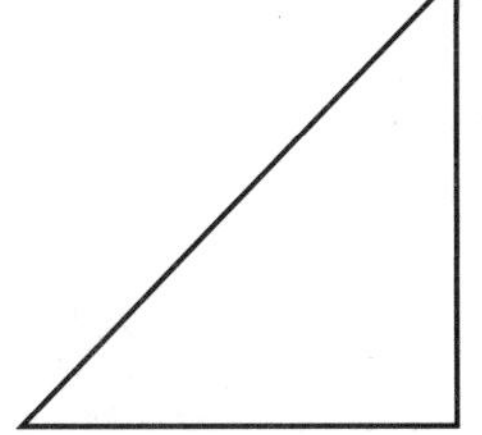

4.

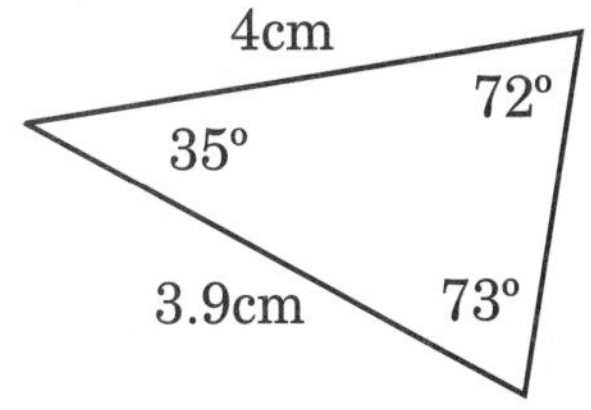

5.

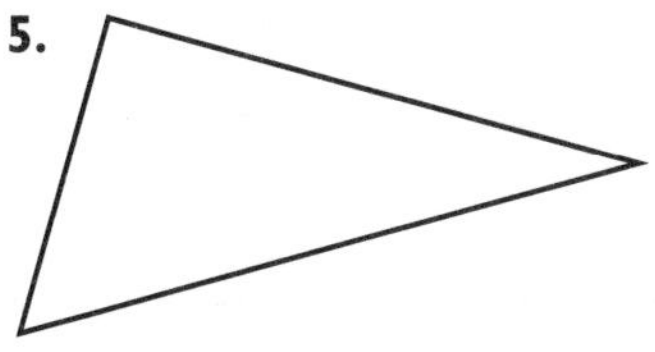

3.

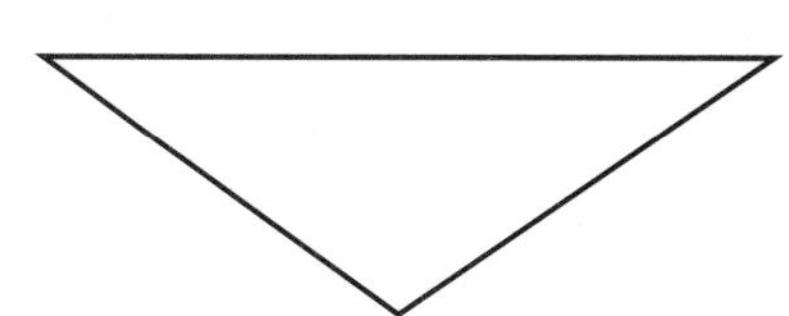

Communicating with Geometrical Figures

Sometimes we want to express ideas more generally in geometry, so we don't want to use specific measurements as we have done so far.

Congruent Sides: ***Small lines are used to show if 2 segments are congruent.***

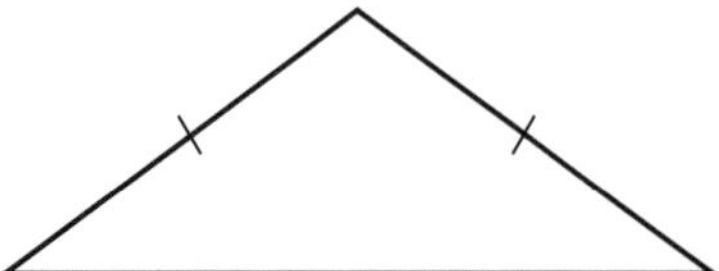

This is an isosceles triangle because 2 sides are shown to be congruent.

Congruent Angles: ***Small arcs are used to show if 2 angles are congruent.***
$\angle E \cong \angle F$ ***because they each have a single arc.***

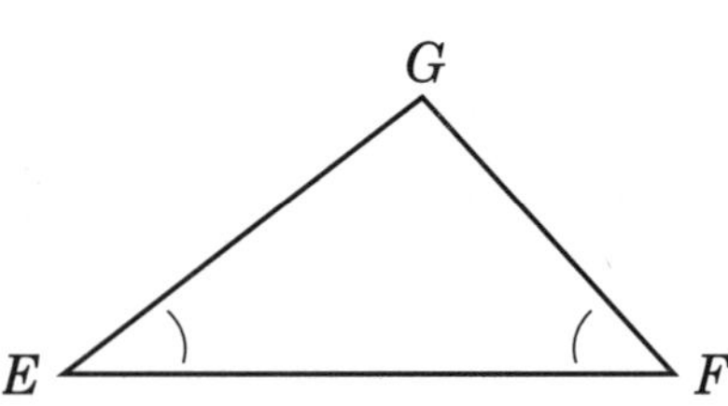

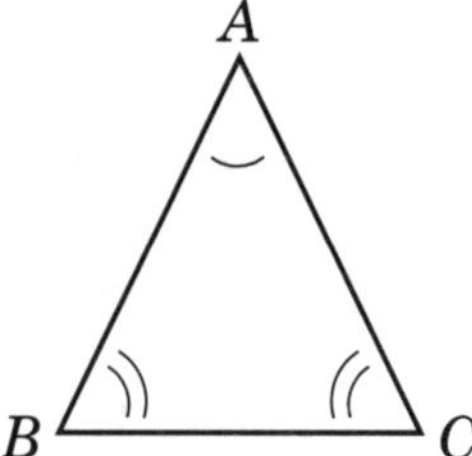

$\angle B$ and $\angle C$ are congruent because they both have double arcs.

They are not congruent to $\angle A$.

Scalene Triangle $\triangle ABC$

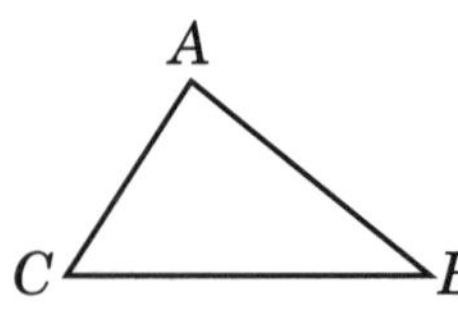

- A, B and C are vertices.
- $\overline{AC}$, $\overline{AB}$ and $\overline{BC}$ are sides.
- There are no congruent parts.

Isosceles Triangle $\triangle DEF$

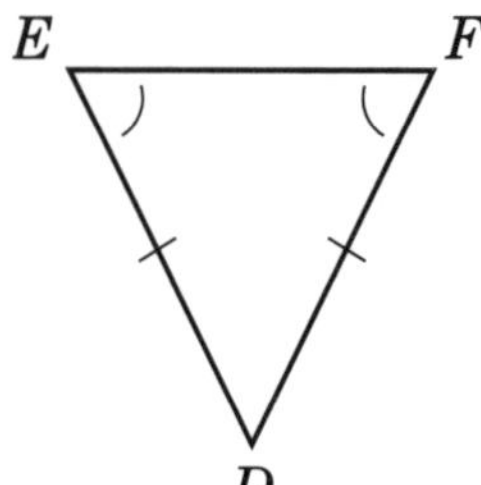

- D, E and F are vertices.
- $\overline{DF}$ and $\overline{DE}$ are congruent and are called the legs.
- $\overline{FE}$ is the base – it is the side that is not congruent. The base does not have to be the bottom of the triangle.
- $\angle F \cong \angle E$ are the base angles.
- $\angle D$ is the vertex angle.

Right Triangle $\triangle GHI$

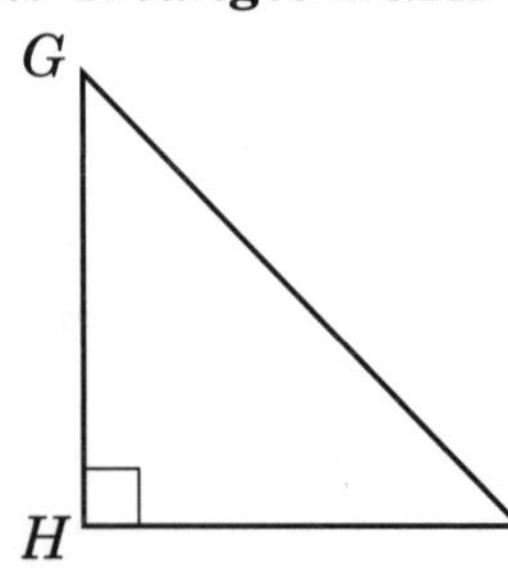

- G, H and I are vertices.
- $\overline{GH}$ and $\overline{HI}$ are the legs. (They do not have to be congruent like the legs of an isosceles triangle.)
- $\overline{GI}$ is the hypotenuse (it is across from the right angle).
- $\angle H$ is the right angle (this is shown by the box).

Practice

Based on the congruent marks, what type of triangle is each?

1. 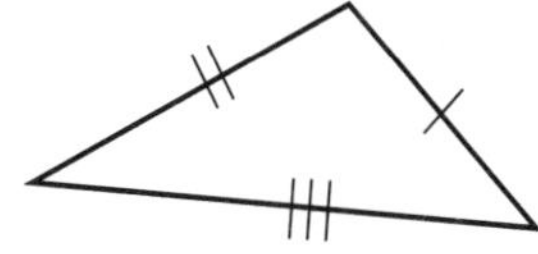

2. 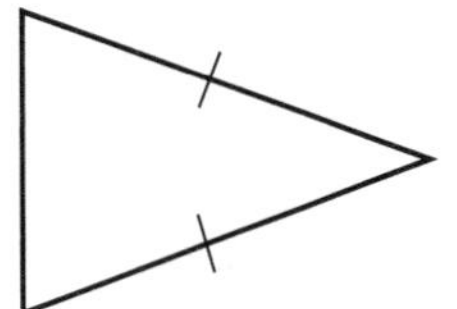

3. 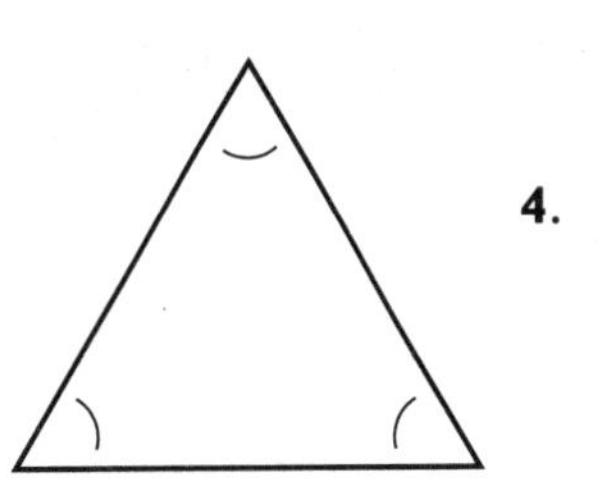

4. 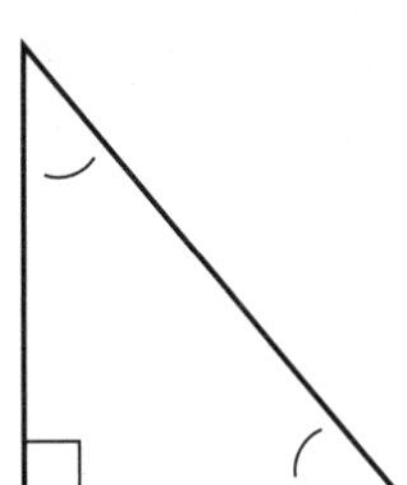

Label the parts of each triangle with the vocabulary for that type of triangle.

5. 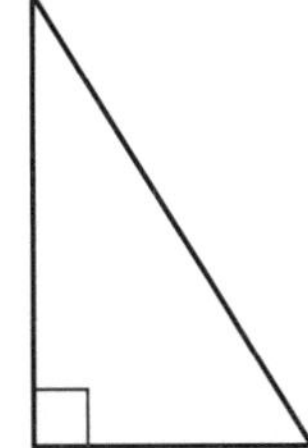

6. 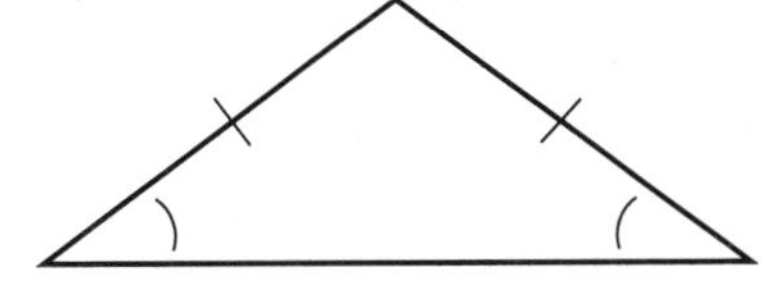

7. 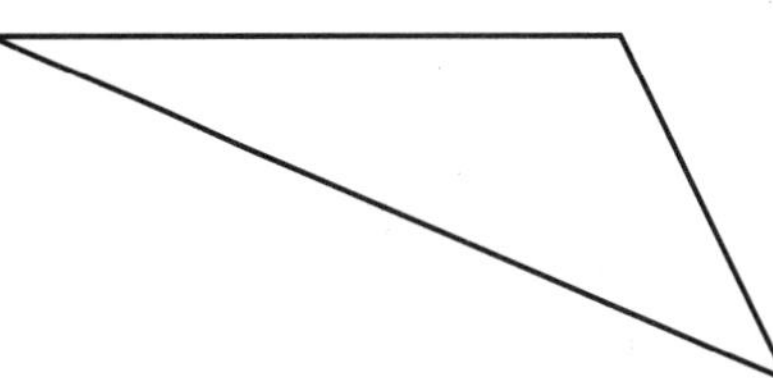

Angle Measurements in Triangles

Since every triangle has 3 angles whose measures total 180°, if we know the measures of 2 angles, we can find the 3rd angle.

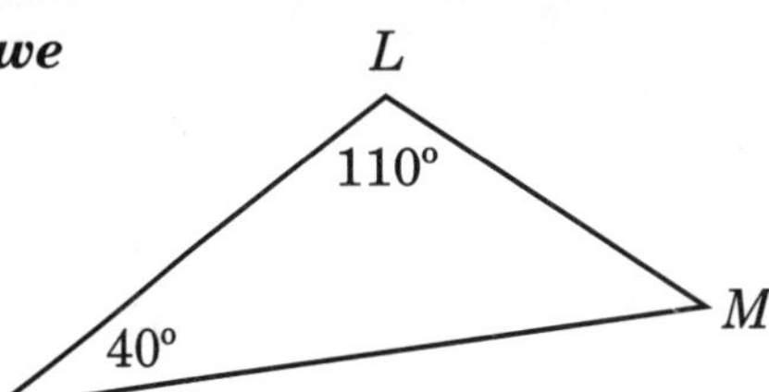

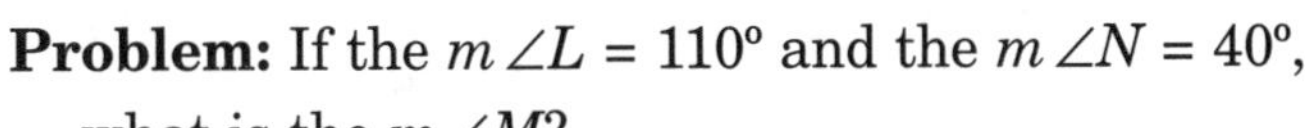
Problem: If the $m\angle L = 110°$ and the $m\angle N = 40°$, what is the $m\angle M$?

Answer: The angles we know make up $110° + 40° = 150°$. That leaves $180° - 150° = 30°$ for the 3rd angle. So $m\angle M = 30°$.

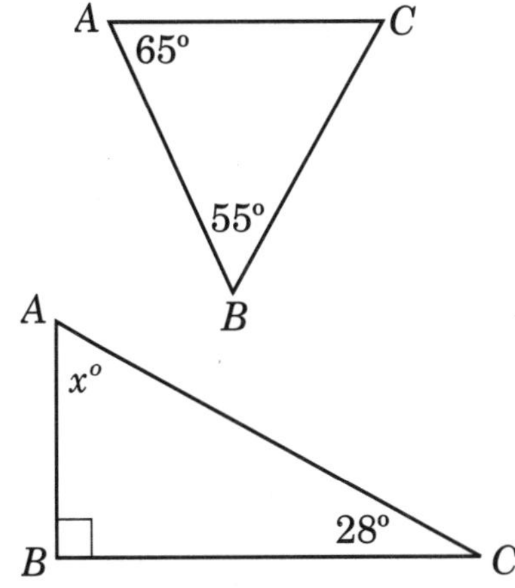

Problem: What is the $m\angle C$?

Answer: The picture shows that $m\angle A + m\angle B = 65° + 55° = 120°$. That leaves $180° - 120° = 60°$. So $m\angle C = 60°$.

The same ideas apply when we combine algebra and geometry.

Problem: $m\angle B = 90°$, $m\angle C = 28°$, $m\angle A = x$. Find x.

Answer: The angles total 180°, so $90° + 28° + x = 180°$

$$118° + x = 180°$$
$$x = 62°$$

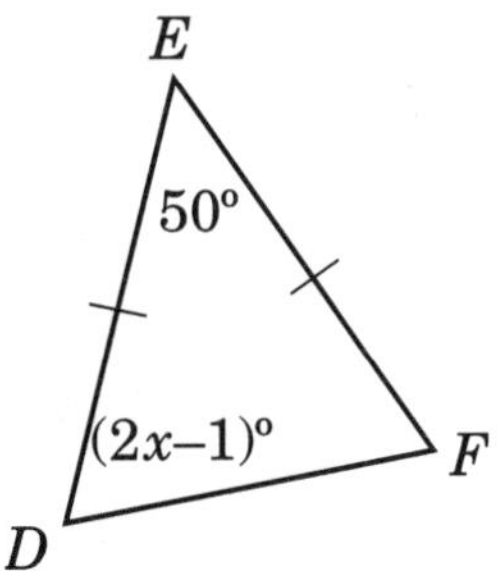

Problem: $m\angle E = 50°$ and $m\angle D = 2x - 1$. Find $m\angle F$.

Answer: We know $m\angle F$ is also $2x - 1$ because $\angle D$ and $\angle F$ are the base angles.

$$50 + 2x - 1 + 2x - 1 = 180$$
$$48 + 4x = 180$$
$$4x = 132$$
$$x = 33°$$

$$m\angle F = 2x - 1$$
$$= 2(33) - 1$$
$$= 66 - 1$$
$$= 65°$$

Practice

For each triangle, find the value of x and/or the measure of any angles that are not given.

1.

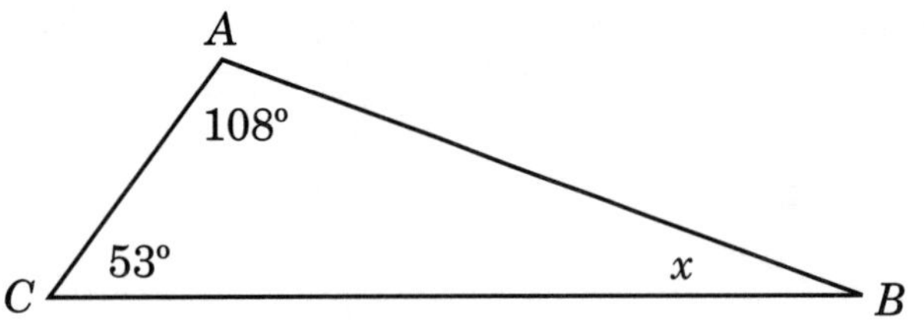

2.

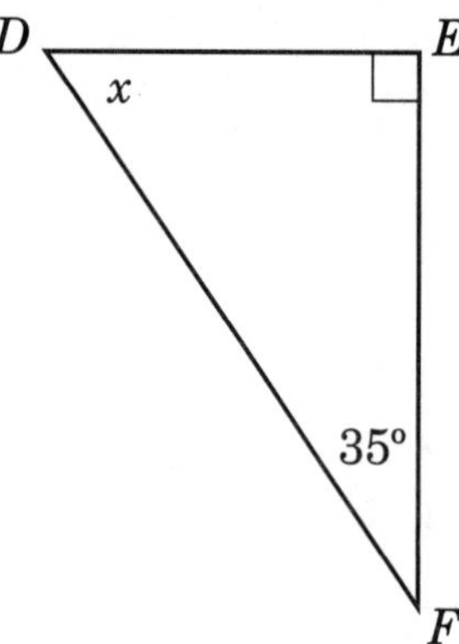

3.

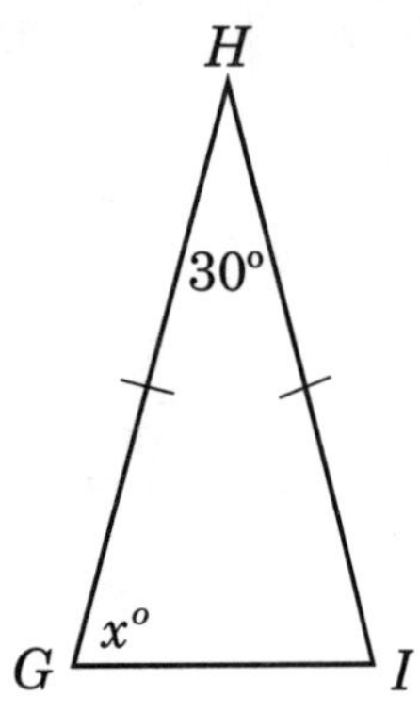

4.

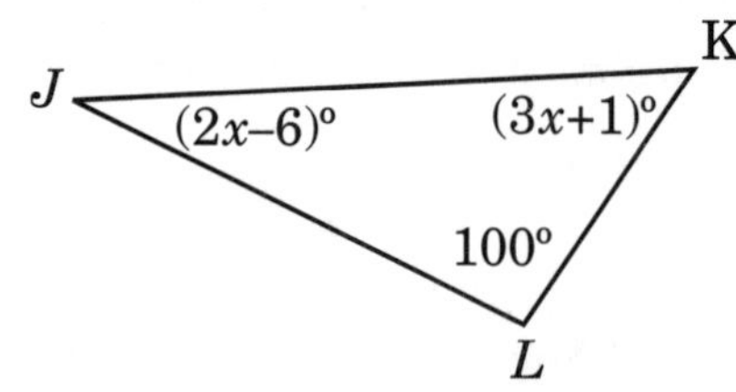

5.

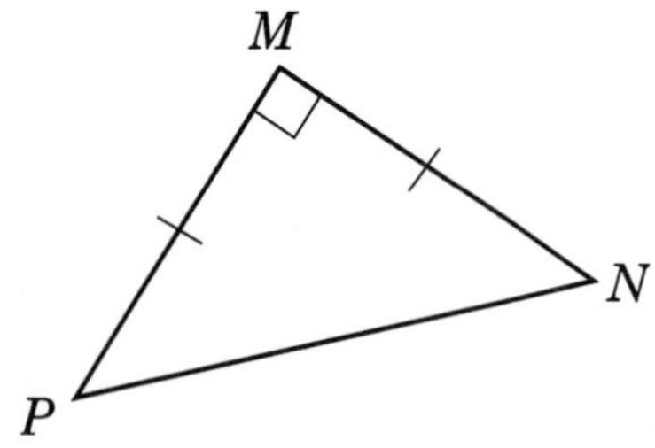

6.

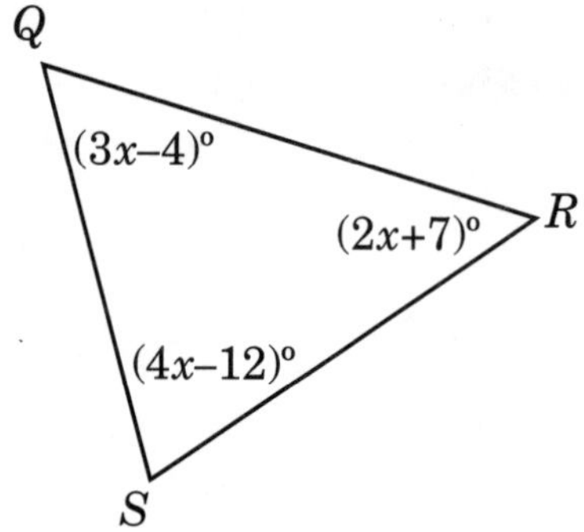

Exterior and Remote Interior Angles

An exterior angle is formed by extending one side of a triangle.

- $\angle B$, $\angle BCA$ and $\angle A$ are interior angles.
- $\angle ACD$ is an exterior angle.
- $\angle A$ and $\angle B$ are the remote interior angles to exterior $\angle ACD$ because they are not adjacent to $\angle ACD$. In other words, $\angle A$ *and* $\angle B$ are the two interior angles farthest from $\angle ACD$.

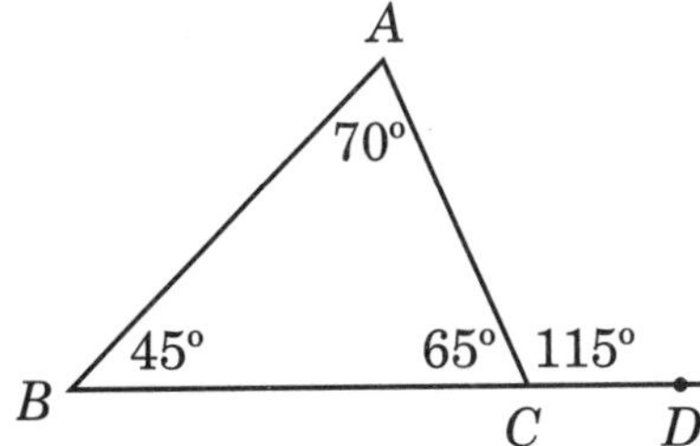

What we should notice...

- Since $\angle ACB$ and $\angle ACD$ form a straight line ($\overline{BD}$), they are supplementary angles. Supplementary angles are an angle pair whose sum is 180°.

- The sum of the remote interior angles is equal to the exterior angle. An informal proof of this fact appears below.

  In a triangle, $m\angle A + m\angle B + m\angle ACB = 180°$.
  Since they make a straight angle,
  $m\angle ACB + m\angle ACD = 180°$.
  Doing some algebraic manipulations:
  $180° - m\angle ACB = m\angle A + m\angle B$
  and $180° - m\angle ACB = m\angle ACD$.
  By substitution, $m\angle A + m\angle B = m\angle ACD$.

- The sum of the exterior angles, one at each vertex of the triangle, is 360°.

  $110° + 120° + 130° = 360°$

  $145° + 65° + 150° = 360°$

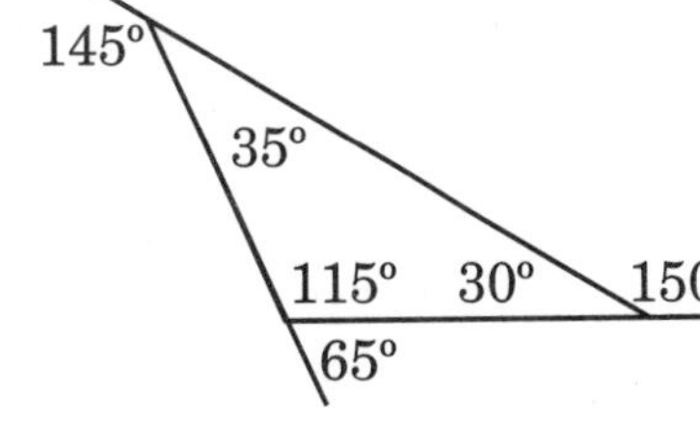

Practice

Find the value of x and/or y in each figure.

1.

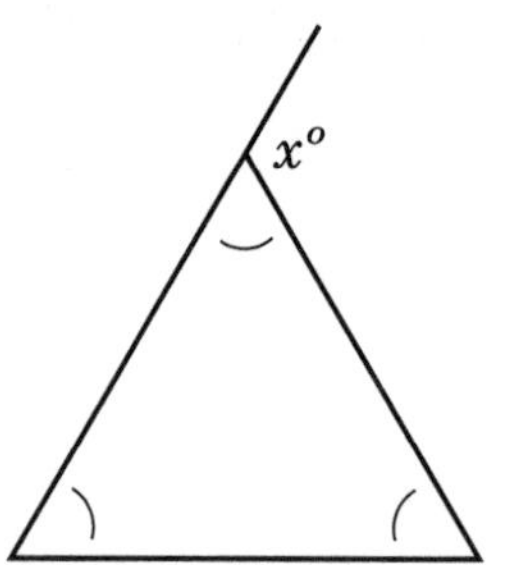

2.

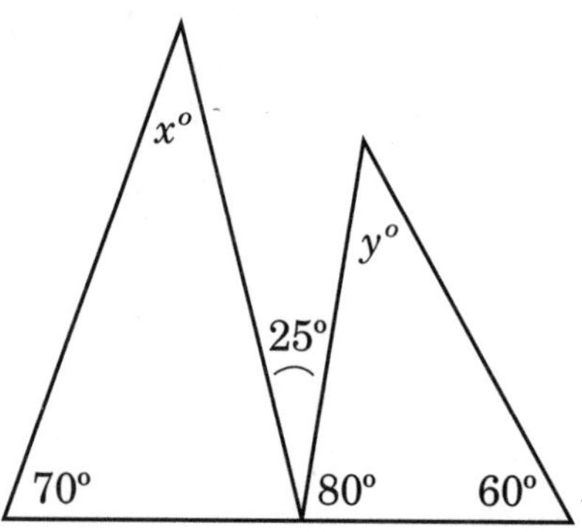

3.

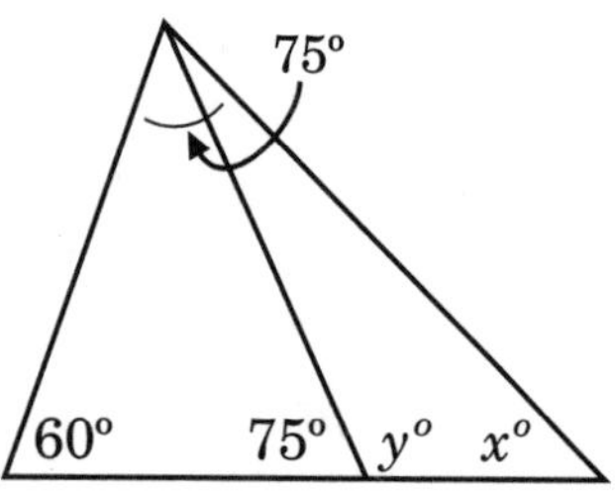

4.

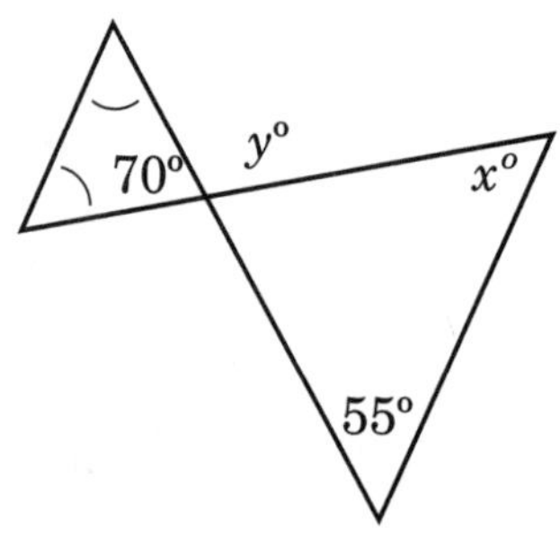

5.

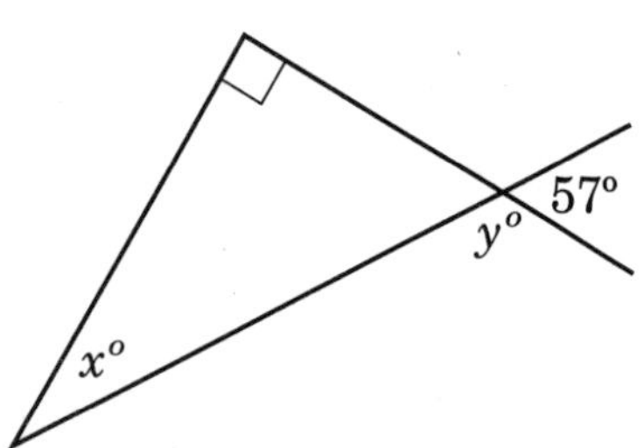

6.

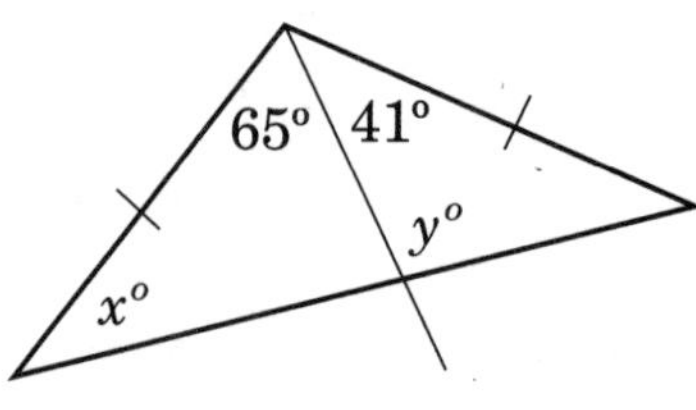

7.

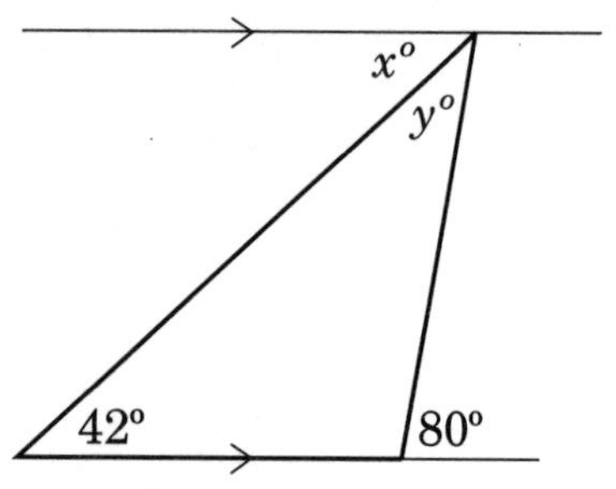

8. This is a parallelogram.

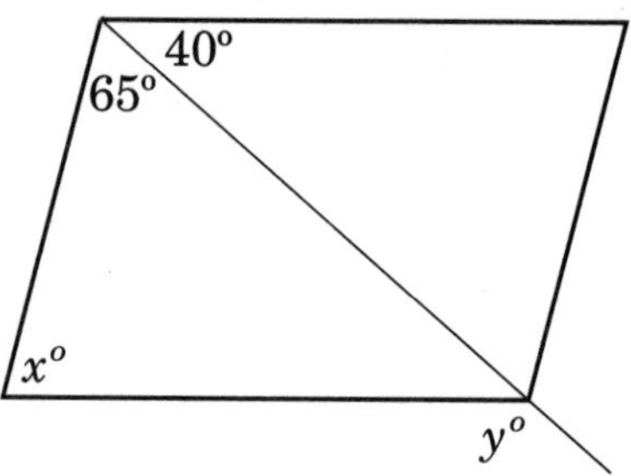

Chapter 2

Right Triangles

The Pythagorean Theorem

The Pythagorean Theorem can be used to find the lengths of the sides of a right triangle.

For right triangle ΔXYZ, $XY = a$, $YZ = b$ and $XZ = c$. $\overline{XY}$ and $\overline{YZ}$ are the legs. $\overline{XZ}$ is the hypotenuse. When using the Pythagorean Theorem, c must <u>always</u> be the length of the hypotenuse.

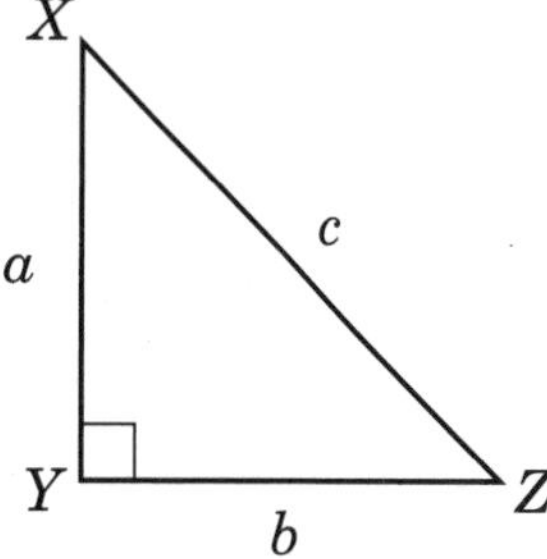

The Pythagorean Theorem provides us with this equation $a^2 + b^2 = c^2$. From this equation, we can find the length of one side if we know the other 2 sides.

Problem: If the legs of a right triangle have lengths of 9 centimeters and 5 centimeters, what is the length of the hypotenuse?

Answer: If we let a and b be the legs and c be the hypotenuse: $a = 9$, $b = 5$ and c = what we're looking for.

$$a^2 + b^2 = c^2$$
$$9^2 + 5^2 = c^2$$
$$81 + 25 = c^2$$
$$106 = c^2$$
$$c = \sqrt{106}$$

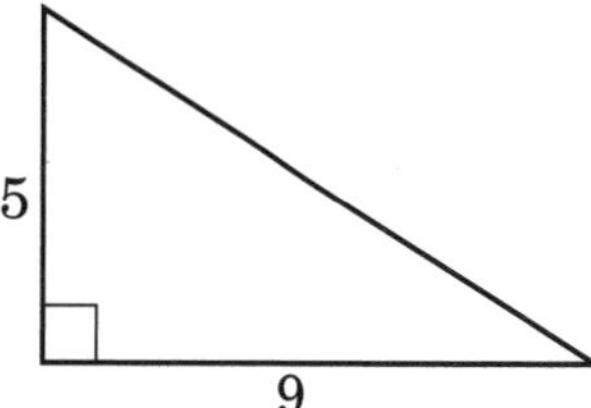

So the length of the hypotenuse is $\sqrt{106}$ cm, which is a bit more than 10cm.

Problem: What is the missing length in ΔRST?

Answer: $ST = a = 8$, $RT = c = 17$, $RS = b$ = what we're looking for.

$$a^2 + b^2 = c^2$$
$$8^2 + b^2 = 172$$
$$64 + b^2 = 289$$
$$b^2 = 225$$
$$b = 15$$

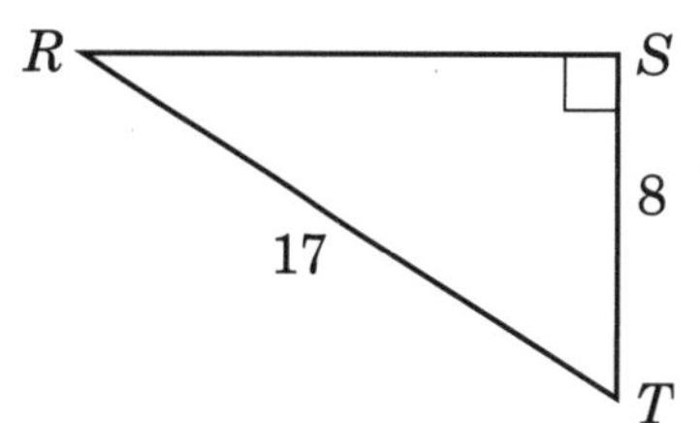

So the missing length is $RS = 15$.

Practice

Find the value of x in each of these right triangles.

1.

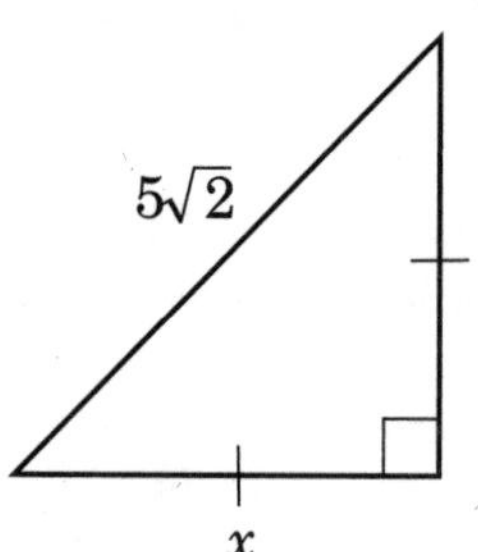

2.

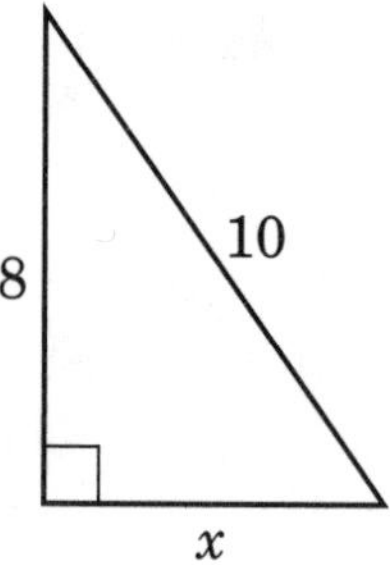

3.

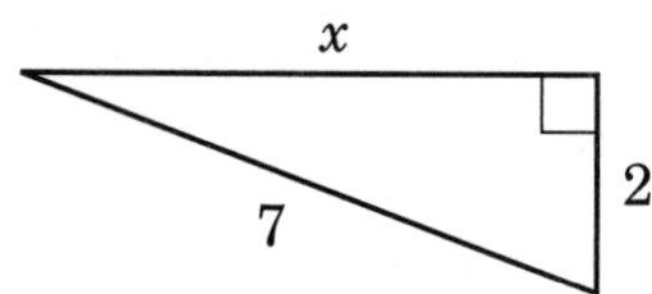

4.

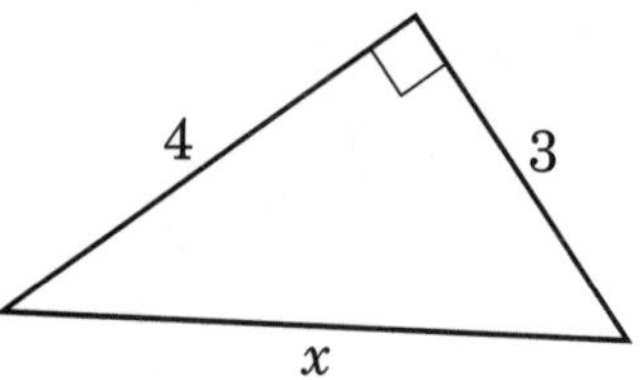

5.

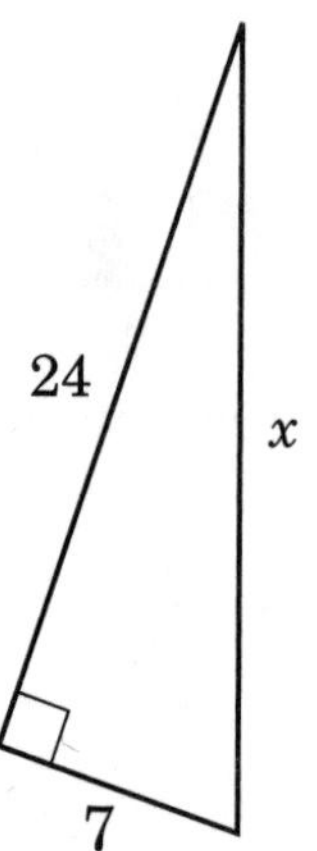

6.

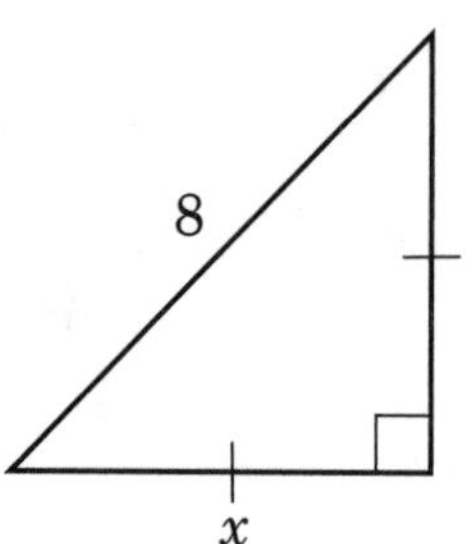

Special Right Triangles

To be a right triangle, the triangle must have 1 right angle. The other two angles are always complementary. We can always use the Pythagorean theorem to find the length of the third side if we know the other two. But there are two special right triangles which have shortcuts for finding the lengths of their sides.

45–45–90 Triangles (Isosceles Right Triangles)

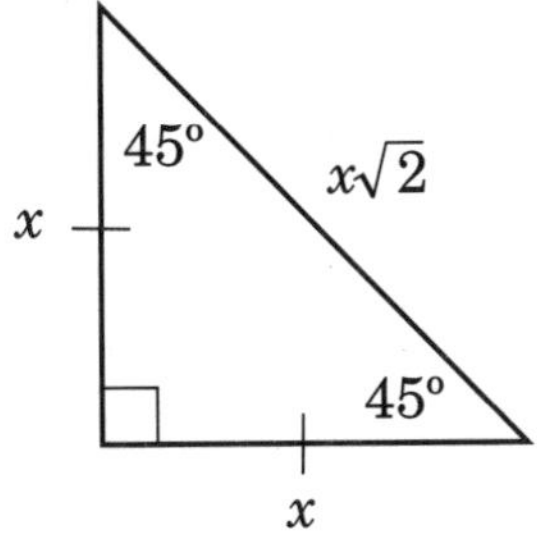

If you know one leg of a 45–45–90 triangle, you automatically know the other leg because they are congruent to each other. But you can find the hypotenuse right away because it will always be $\sqrt{2}$ times the length of the leg.

30–60–90 Triangles

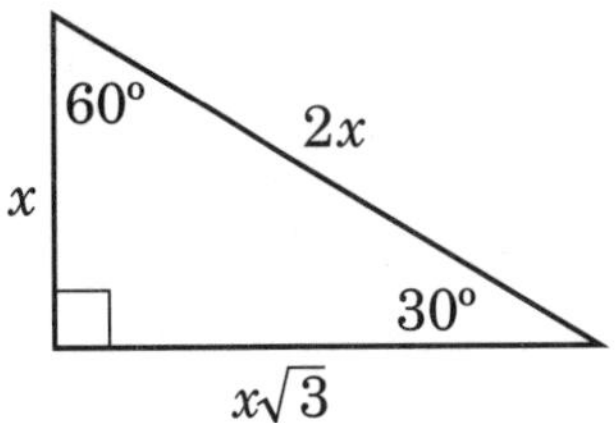

If you know the length of the shortest leg in a 30–60–90 triangle, you can find the longer leg by multiplying the length of the shorter leg by $\sqrt{3}$. You can find the length of the hypotenuse by doubling the shorter leg.

Note: the shortest side is always opposite the 30° angle.

Problem: Find the length of the hypotenuse of ΔABC.

Answer: If $m\angle B = 90$ and $m\angle C = 60$, $m\angle A$ must be 30 because the sum of the angles is 180°. Since this is a 30–60–90 triangle and we know $\overline{BC}$ is the shortest leg, we can use the pattern to find the other two lengths.

So, $AB = BC\sqrt{3} = 3\sqrt{3}$, and $AC = 2BC = 2 \cdot 3 = 6$.

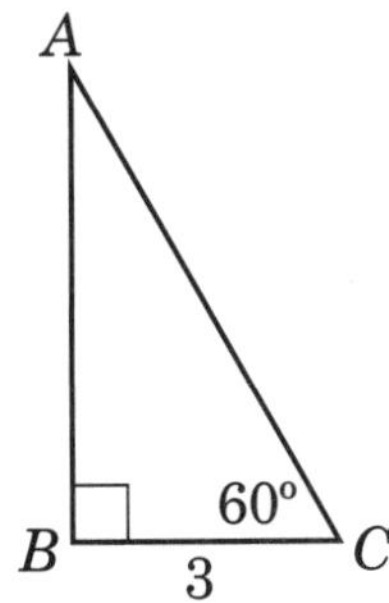

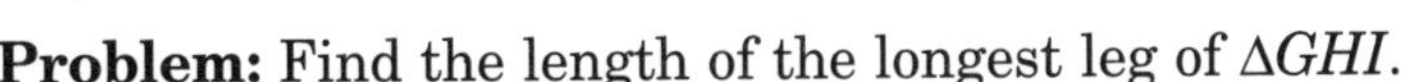

Problem: Find the length of the longest leg of ΔGHI.

Answer: The pattern for a 30–60–90 triangle is based on the shortest leg. First we need to find the length of the shortest leg. Since, according to the pattern $GI = 2 \cdot HI$, we can substitute into and solve this equation: $10 = 2(GI$

$$\frac{10}{2} = \frac{2GT}{2}$$

$$5 = GI$$

Once we know the length of the shortest leg, we can find the longest leg by multiplying the shortest leg by $\sqrt{3}$: $5 \cdot \sqrt{3} = 5\sqrt{3}$. So, $GH = 5\sqrt{3}$.

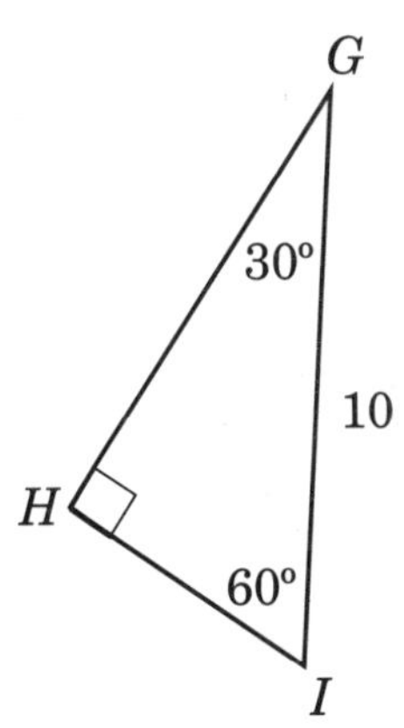

Problem: Find the length of the hypotenuse of ΔDEF.

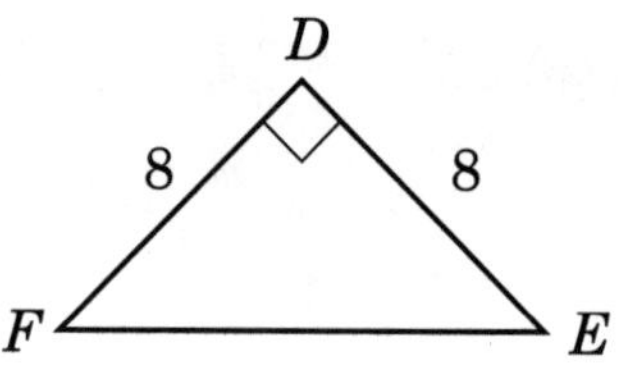

Answer: Since ΔDEF is an isosceles right triangle, it is a 45–45–90 triangle, so the first pattern applies. Each of the legs has a length of 8, so the hypotenuse is $\sqrt{2}$ times 8. $FE = 8\sqrt{2}$.

Problem: What is the value of x in ΔJKL?

Answer: The pattern says that the length of the hypotenuse is equal to the length of the leg times $\sqrt{2}$ in a 45–45–90 triangle. Remember this is an isosceles right triangle. So:

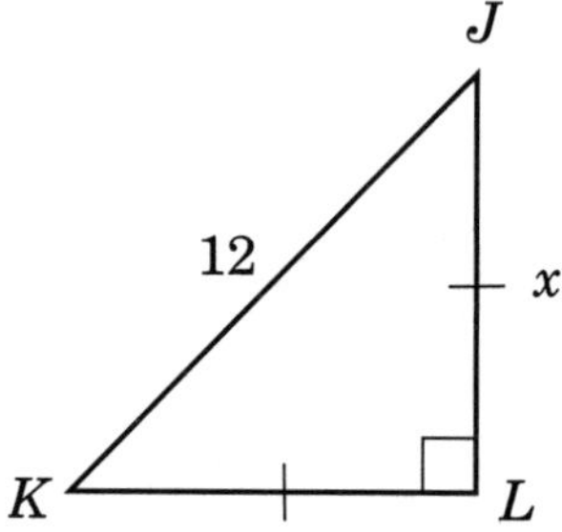

$$KJ = JL\sqrt{2}$$
$$12 = x\sqrt{2}$$
$$\frac{12}{\sqrt{2}} = \frac{x\sqrt{2}}{2}$$
$$x = \frac{12}{\sqrt{2}}$$

But we can't leave a radical in the denominator, so we have to rationalize the denominator to get the final answer:

$$x = \frac{12}{\sqrt{2}} \cdot \frac{\sqrt{2}}{\sqrt{2}}$$
$$x = \frac{12\sqrt{2}}{2}$$
$$x = 6\sqrt{2}$$

Practice

Find the value of x and/or y in each figure.

1.

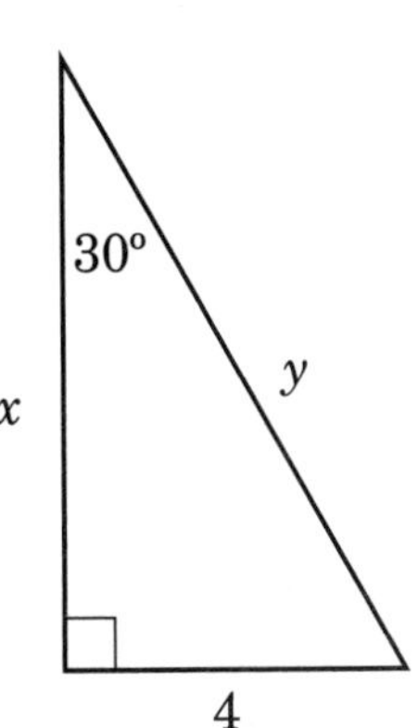

2.

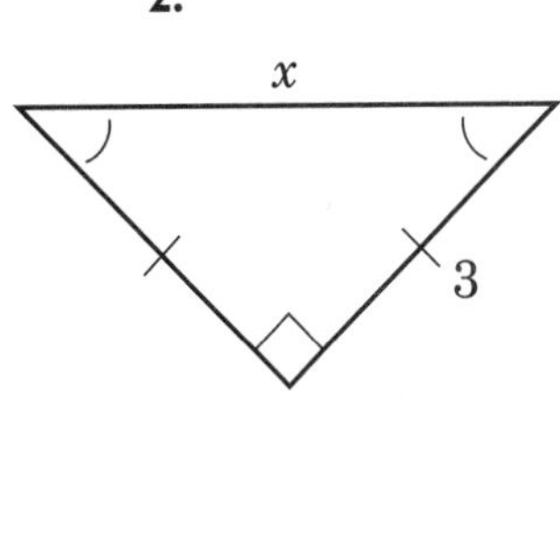

3. *RSTU* is a square.

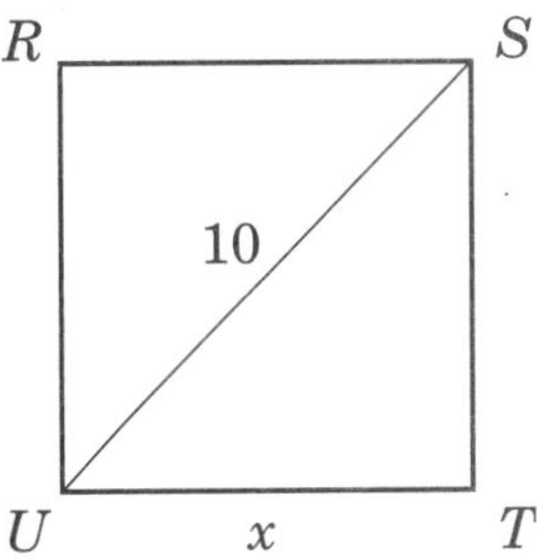

4. *ABCD* is a rectangle.

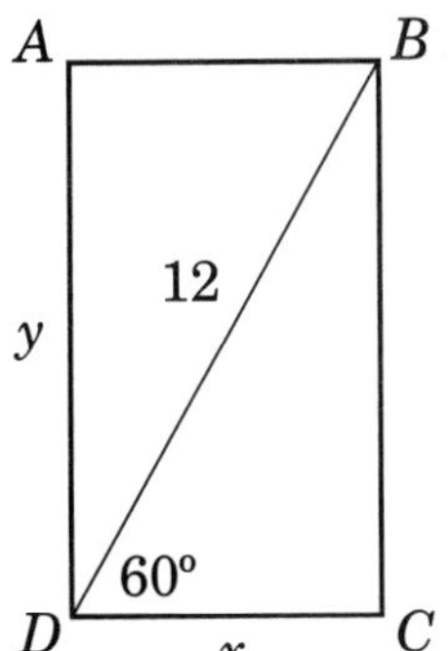

5. $\overline{MP}$ is an altitude. $LN = 12$
$m\angle LMN = 60°$

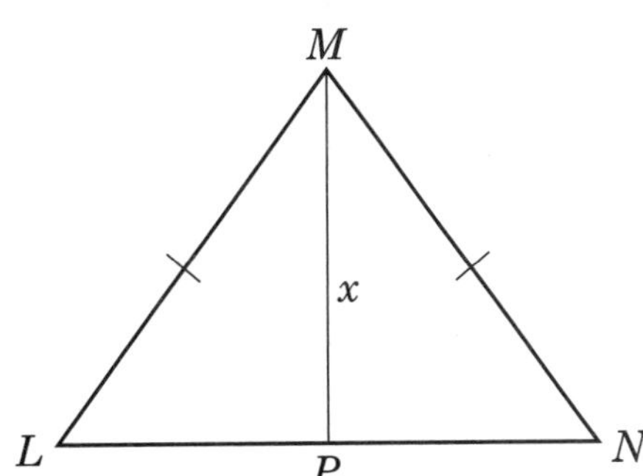

6. $m\angle GFE = 105°$

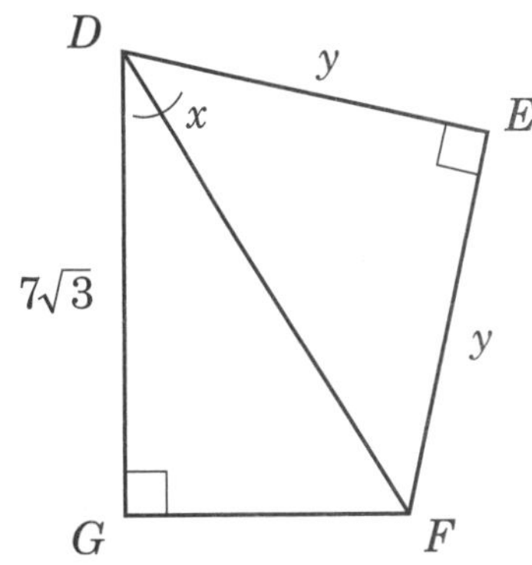

Chapter 3

Perimeter and Area

What Is Perimeter?

The perimeter of a triangle is the distance around it. To find the perimeter, add the lengths of the sides together. Note: $\overline{AC}$ is read "segment AC" or "side AC" while AC, *with no symbol,* is read "the length of AC."

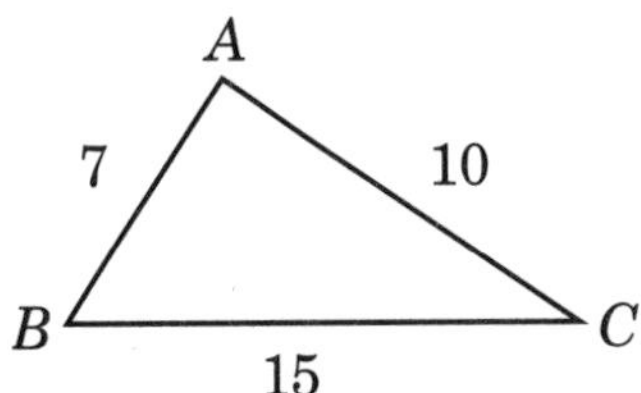

Problem: What is the perimeter of ΔABC?

Answer: From the picture we can see that $AC = 10$, $CB = 15$ and $BA = 7$. The perimeter of ΔABC is the sum of the lengths of these sides.

$10 + 15 + 7 = 32$.

The perimeter is 32.

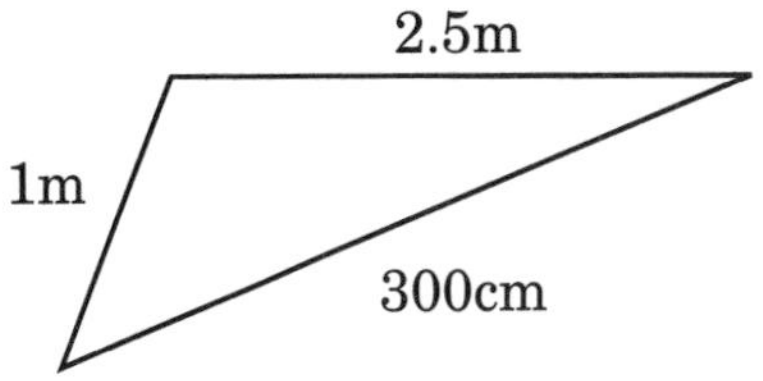

Problem: What is the perimeter of this triangle?

Answer: From the picture we can see that the sides have lengths of 1 meter, 2.5 meters and 300 centimeters. In order to add them together, we first have to convert them to the same unit of measurement. Since there are 100cm in 1 meter, the 1 meter side has a length of 100cm and the 2.5 meter side has a length of 250cm.

100cm + 250cm + 300cm = 650cm.

The perimeter is 650cm or 6.5 meters.

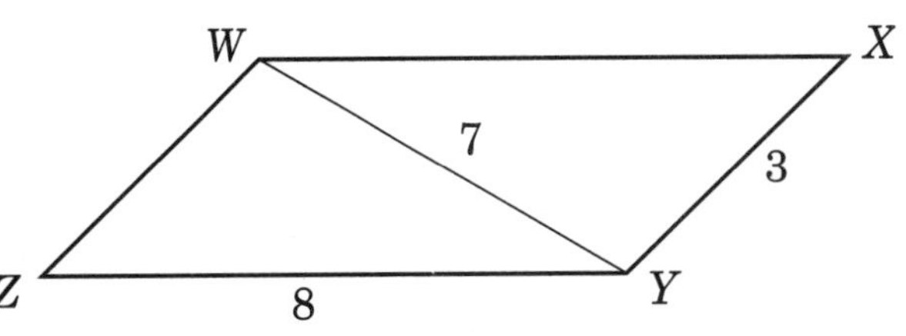

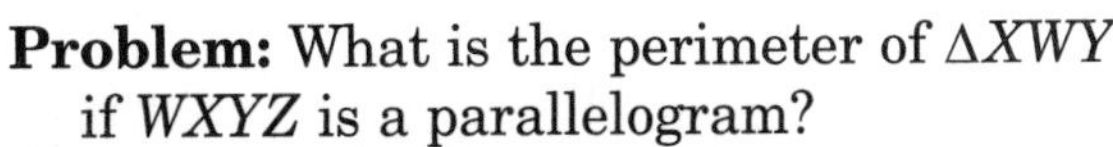

Problem: What is the perimeter of ΔXWY if $WXYZ$ is a parallelogram?

Answer: In a parallelogram, the opposite sides are congruent. Since $XY = 3$, $WZ = 3$. Since $YZ = 8$, $XW = 8$. Therefore, the sides of ΔXWY are $XW = 8$, $WY = 7$ and $XY = 3$. $8 + 7 + 3 = 18$.

The perimeter of ΔXWY is 18.

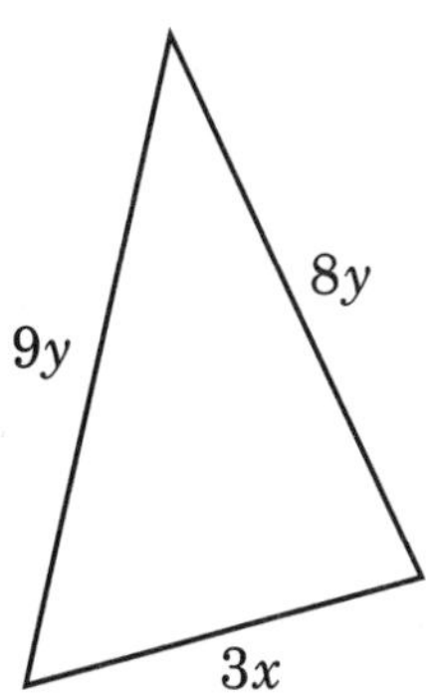

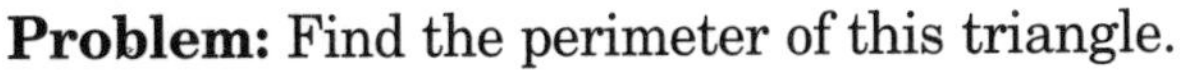

Problem: Find the perimeter of this triangle.

Answer: The sides of this triangle have lengths $3x$, $8y$ and $9y$. $3x + 8y + 9y = 3x + 17y$.

The perimeter is $3x + 17y$.

Remember that you can only combine like terms.

Practice *Find the perimeter of each triangle.*

1.

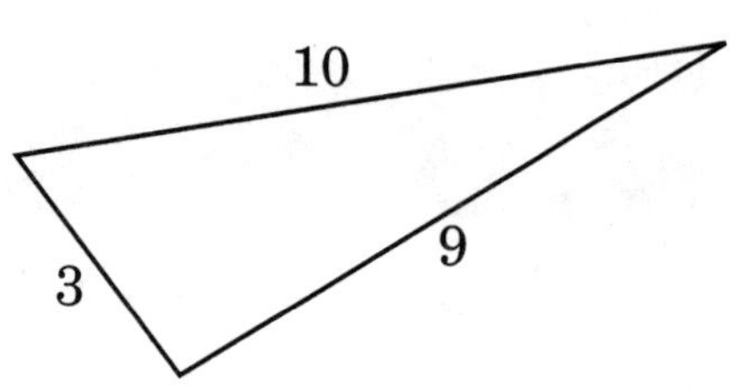

2. $AB = 8$ $AC = 5$

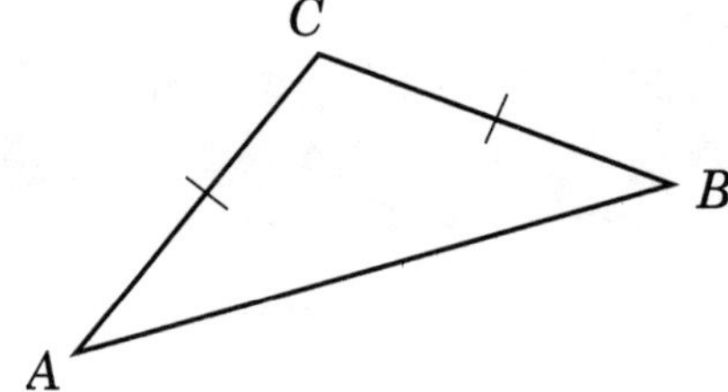

3.

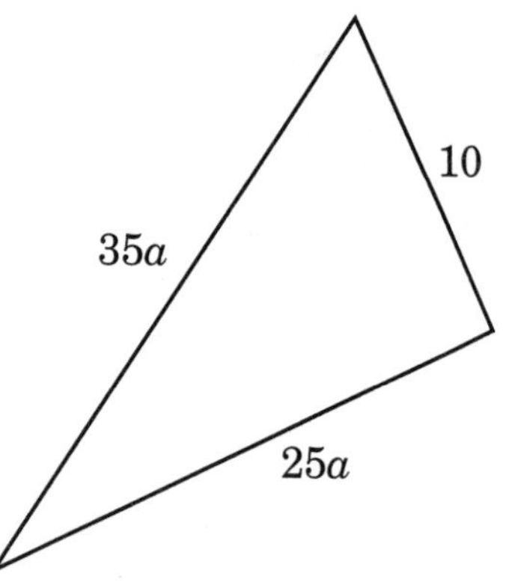

4. Given that $GHIJ$ is a parallelogram, find the perimeter of ΔGIJ.

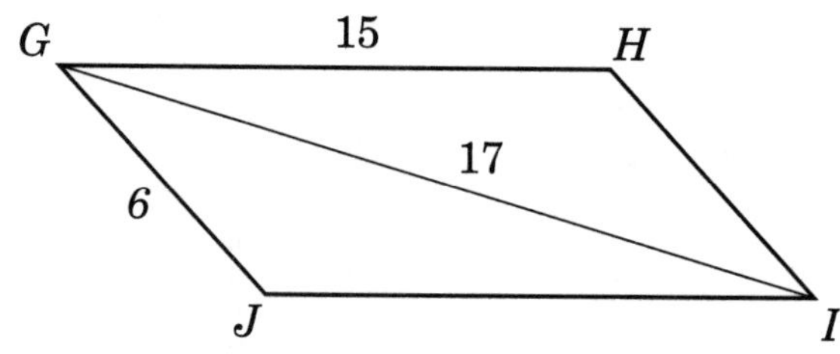

5.

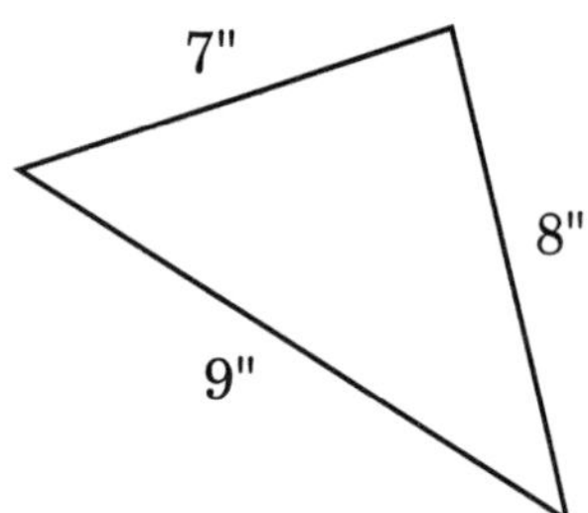

6.

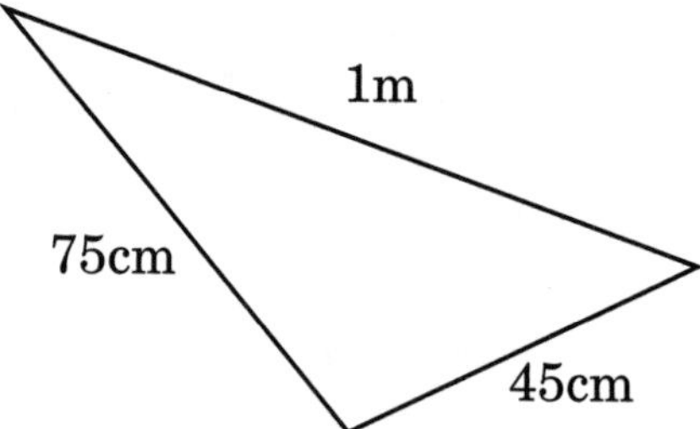

7. Find the perimeter of ΔADC, ΔADB and ΔACB.

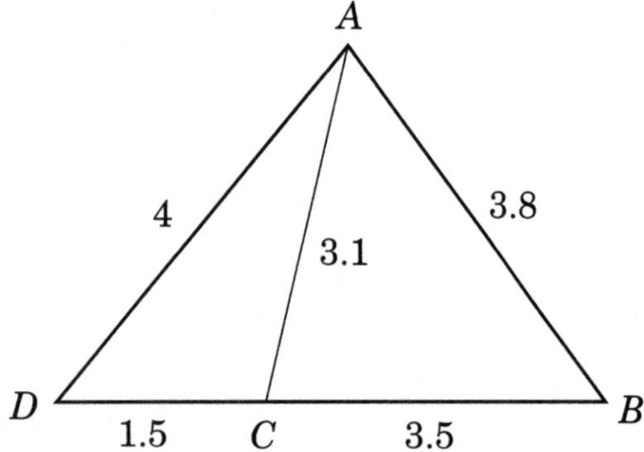

8. If the perimeter of ΔXYZ is 27, what is the length of $\overline{YZ}$?

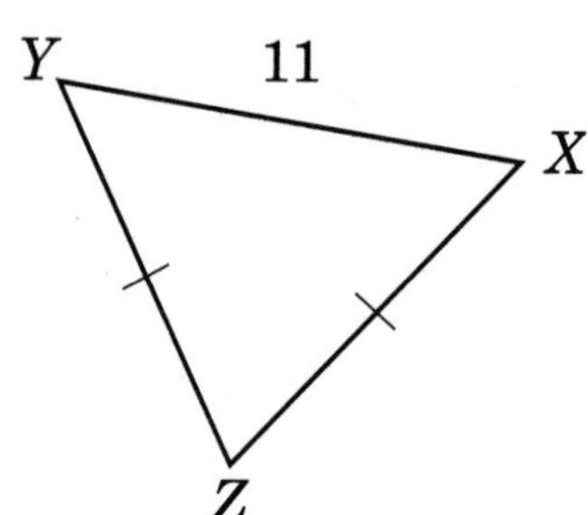

What Is Area?

The area of a triangle is the number of square units it would take to cover the triangle (think about the square tiles on a floor… the number of tiles there are indicates the area of the floor).

$A = \frac{1}{2}bh$ "Area equals one half of the base times the height."

When finding the area of a triangle, any side of a triangle can be a base for the purposes of this formula. Once the base has been chosen, a line is drawn from the opposite vertex perpendicular to the chosen base. This line is called the height, or altitude, of the triangle.

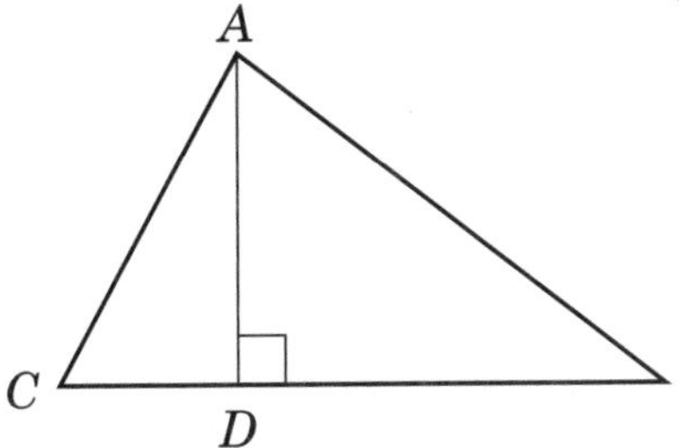

In $\triangle ABC$ $\overline{CB}$ is the base and $\overline{AD}$ is the height.

In $\triangle EFD$, $\overline{DF}$ is the base and $\overline{EG}$ is the height.

- If $\overline{DE}$ was chosen as the base, the height is found by extending an auxiliary line from the base. Then a new perpendicular segment can be drawn from F to the auxiliary line. $\overline{FH}$ then becomes the height. The area of the triangle would be the same, no matter how it was calculated.

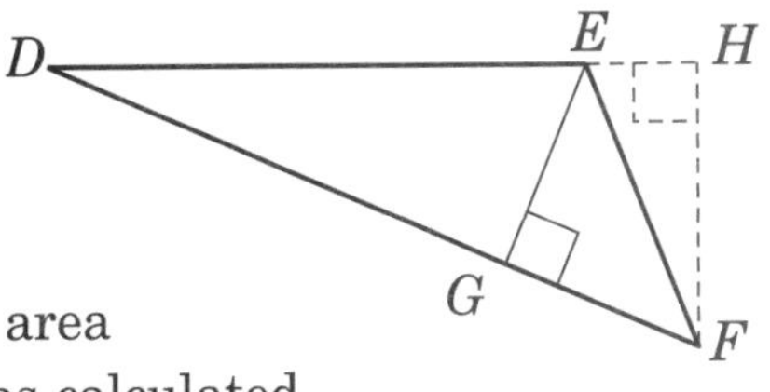

To find the area of a triangle:

1. Find the measures of the base and height.
2. Substitute the values into the formula $A = \frac{1}{2}bh$.
3. Solve.

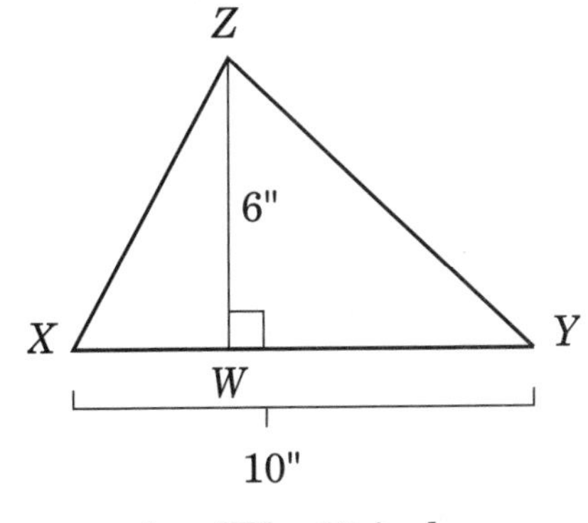

$b = XY = 10$ inches
$h = ZW = 6$ inches
$A = \frac{1}{2}bh$
$= \frac{1}{2} \cdot 10" \cdot 6"$
$= 30\text{in}^2$

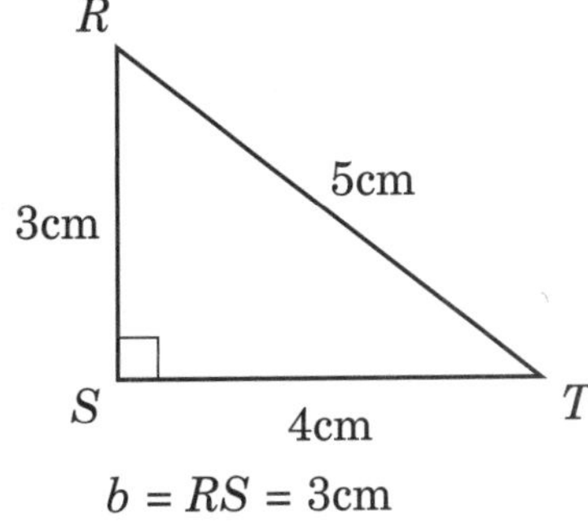

$b = RS = 3\text{cm}$
$h = ST = 4\text{cm}$
$A = \frac{1}{2}bh$
$= \frac{1}{2} \cdot 3\text{cm} \cdot 4\text{cm}$
$= 6\text{cm}^2$

In a right triangle, the height is one leg and the base is the other leg.

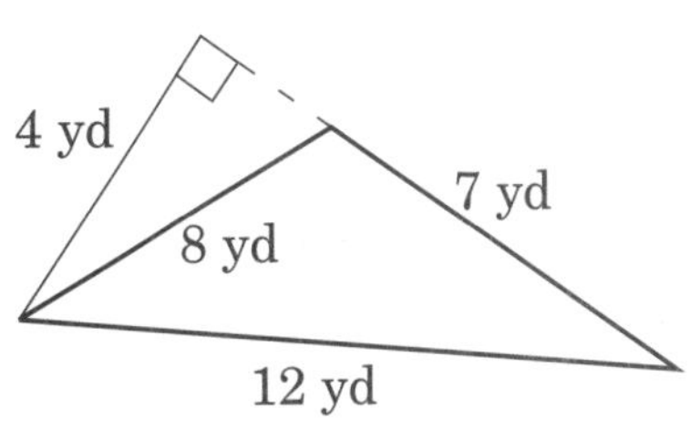

$b = 7$ yards
$h = 4$ yards
$A = \frac{1}{2}bh$
$= \frac{1}{2} \cdot 7\text{yd} \cdot 4\text{yd}$
$= 14\text{yd}^2$

Note: Because area is measured in square units, when you multiply inches by inches, you get in^2. Likewise, centimeters become cm^2, miles become miles^2, etc.

Practice

1. *Find the area of △ABC.*

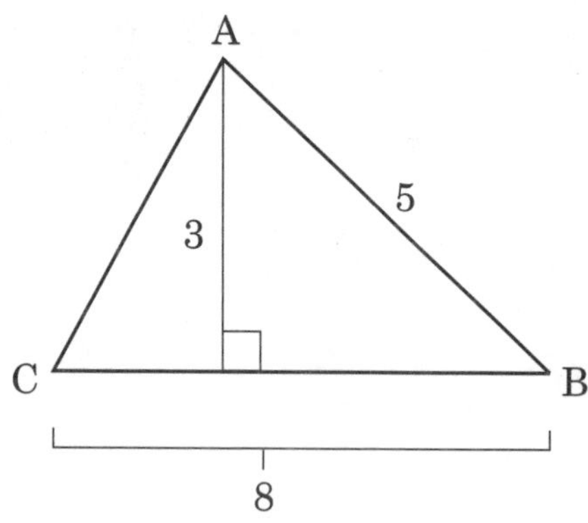

2.

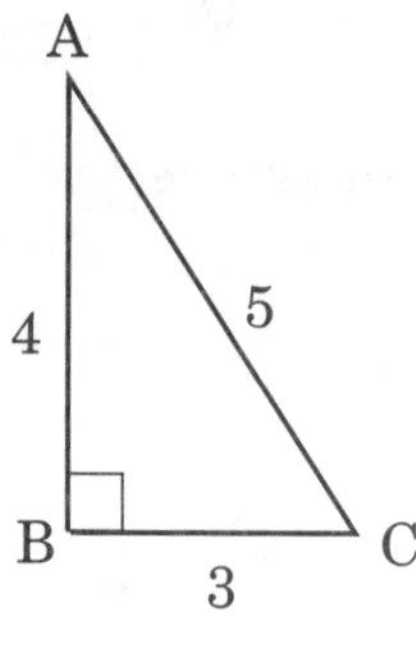

3. *ABCD* is a rectangle.

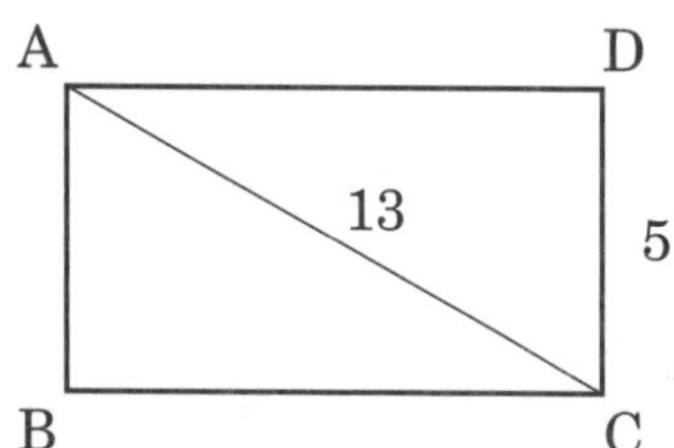

4.

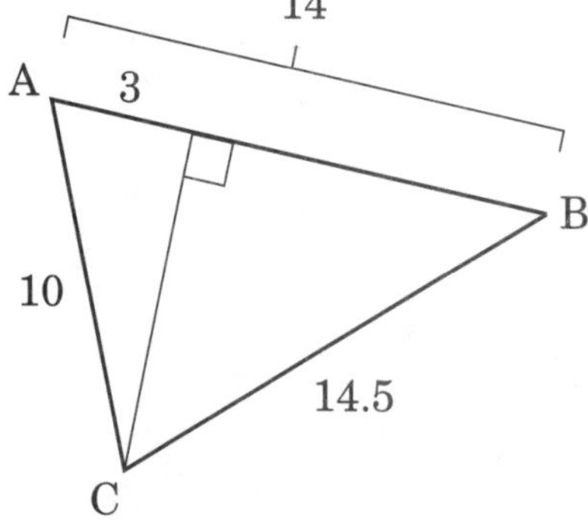

5.

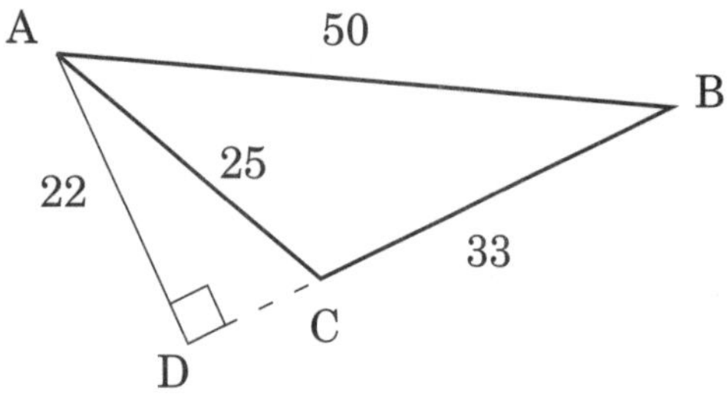

6. *ABCD* is a rhombus.

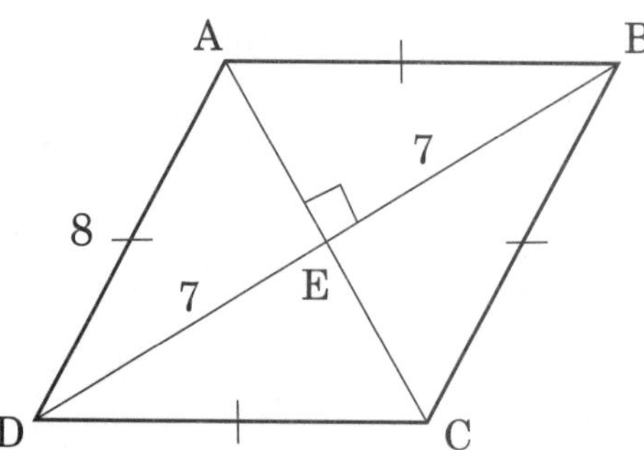

7.

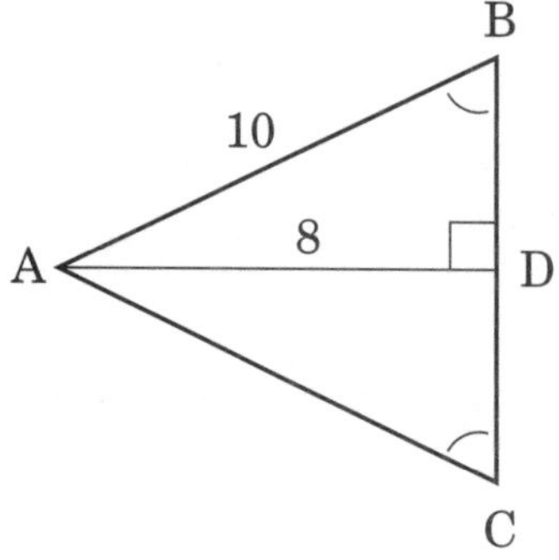

8.

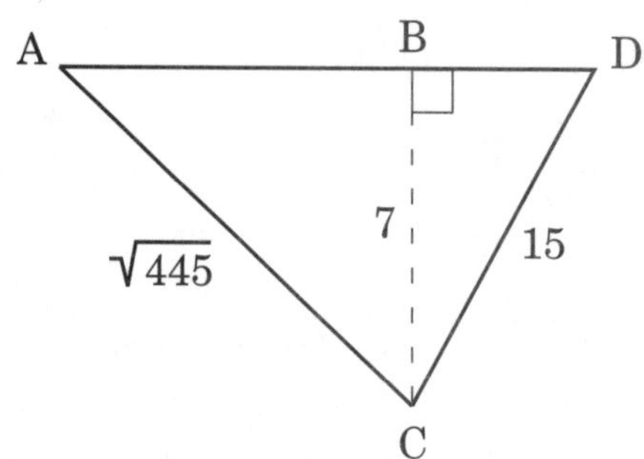

Chapter 4

Special Segments

Segment Definitions

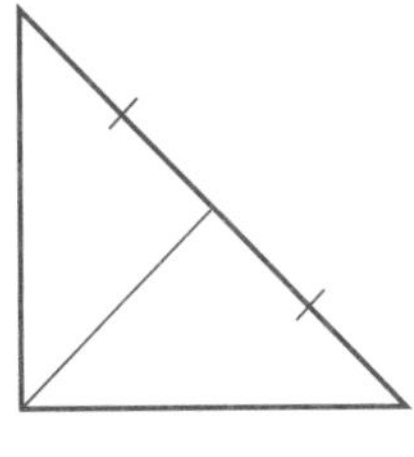

Median

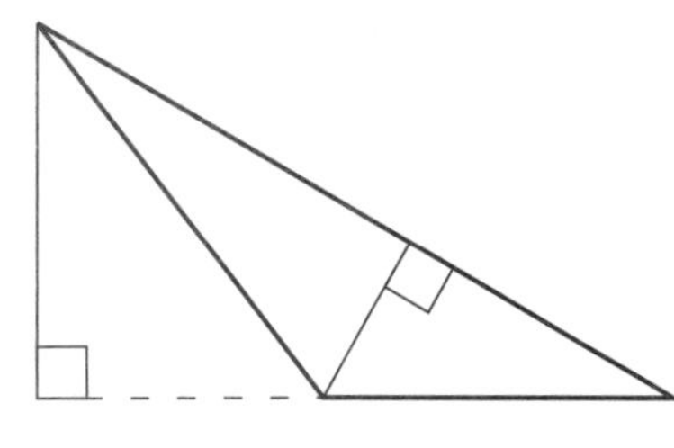

Altitude

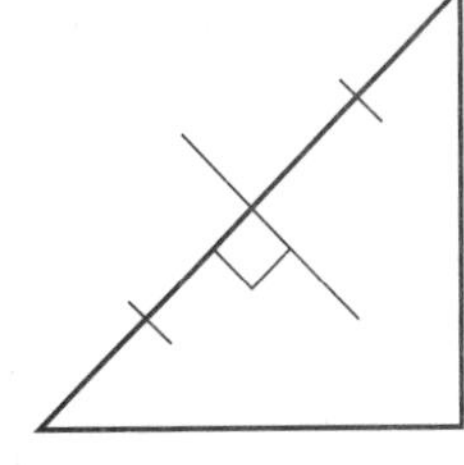

Perpendicular Bisector

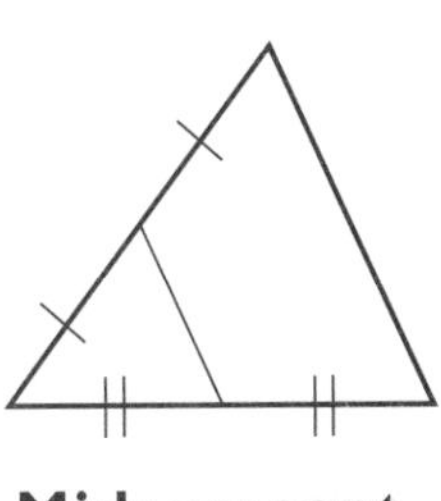

Midsegment

Median: The median of a triangle connects a vertex of the triangle to the midpoint of the opposite side.

- The phrase "opposite side" is often used in the discussion of triangles. The side opposite a vertex is the side which does not touch that vertex.

Vertex	A	B	C
Opposite Side	$\overline{CB}$	$\overline{AC}$	$\overline{AB}$

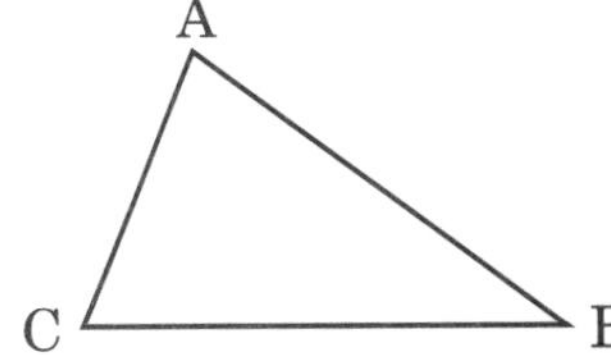

Altitude: The altitude of a triangle is a perpendicular segment from a vertex to the line that contains the opposite side. Sometimes the altitude from a vertex is outside the triangle and an auxiliary line must be drawn to extend the side to meet the altitude.

Perpendicular Bisector: The perpendicular bisector of a triangle is a perpendicular segment that passes through the midpoint of that side.

Midsegment: It is the segment which connects the midpoints of 2 sides of a triangle.

Special Segment	Shortcut Definition
Median	vertex → midpoint
Altitude	vertex → opposite side, forming a right angle
Midsegment	midpoint → midpoint
Perpendicular Bisector	perpendicular segment at the midpoint of a side

Remember: There are 3 of each of these segments in every triangle. There can be one altitude and median from each of the 3 vertices. There can be midsegments connecting any two sides. There can be a perpendicular bisector on each of the 3 sides.

Drawing Special Segments

Median

1. Pick the vertex.
2. Use a ruler to find the midpoint of the opposite side (Point *M*).
3. Use a ruler as a straightedge to connect the midpoint and the vertex.

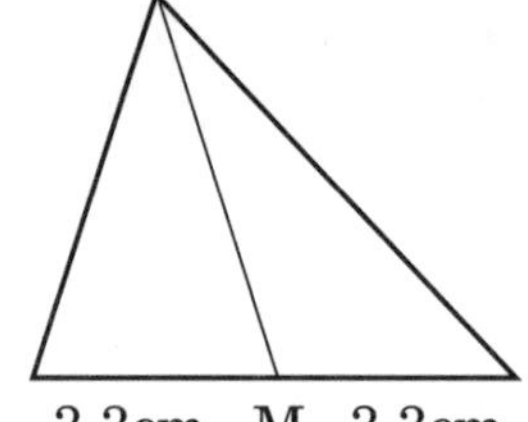

Altitude – Acute Triangle

1. Pick the vertex (Point *A*).
2. Lay a protractor on the triangle so that the 0°-line is lined up with the opposite side.
3. Slide the protractor along the line until the 90°-line points at the vertex.
4. Make a point either in the small hole in your protractor or below the end of the 90°-line (Point *P*).
5. Use a ruler as a straightedge to connect the vertex and the point you made in Step 4.

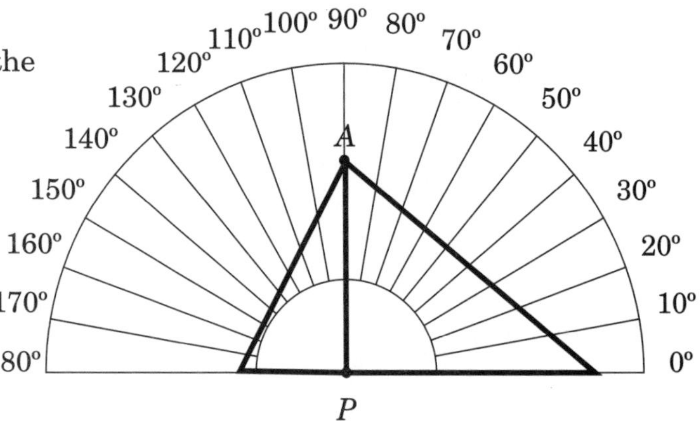

Altitude – Obtuse Triangle

1. Pick the vertex (not the one at the obtuse angle because that one works the same as in an acute triangle), Point *A*.
2. Use a ruler to draw an auxiliary line which extends the opposite side past the obtuse angle.
3. Lay a protractor on the triangle so that the 0°-line is lined up with the opposite side.
4. Slide the protractor along the line until the 90°-line points at the vertex.
5. Make a point either in the small hole in your protractor or below the end of the 90°-line (Point *P*).
6. Use a ruler as a straightedge to connect the vertex and the point you made in Step 5.

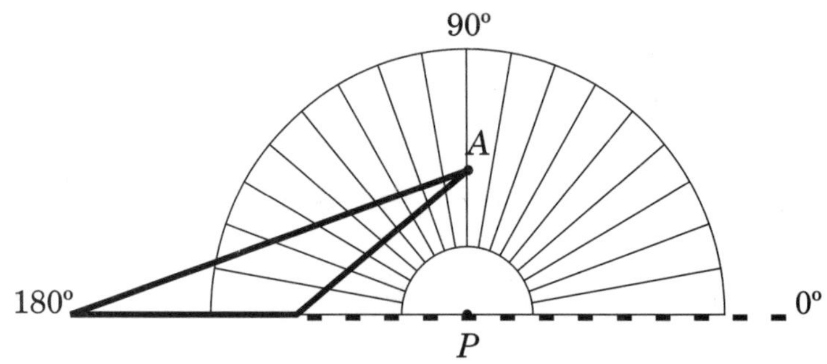

Midsegment

1. Use a ruler to find the midpoints of 2 sides (*X* and *Y*).
2. Use a ruler as a straightedge to connect the 2 midpoints you found in Step 1.

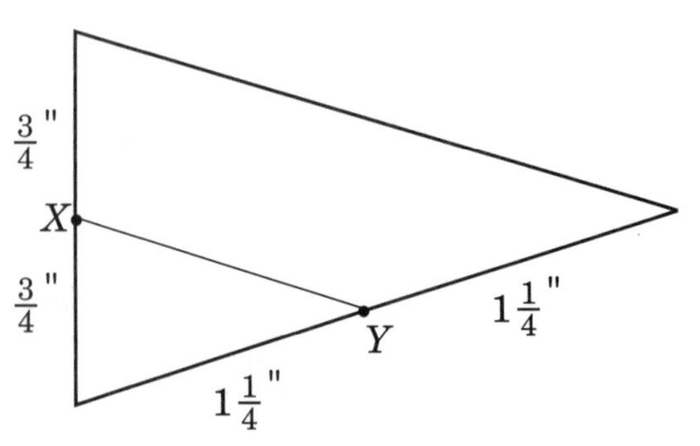

Perpendicular Bisector

1. Pick a side of the triangle.
2. Use a ruler to find the midpoint of the side (Point M).
3. Lay a protractor on the triangle so that the 0°-line of the protractor is lined up with the side.
4. Slide the protractor along the line until the 90°-line passes through the midpoint of the side.
5. Make a point above the 90°-line (Point P).
6. Use a ruler as a straightedge to connect the midpoint of the side with the point made in Step 5.

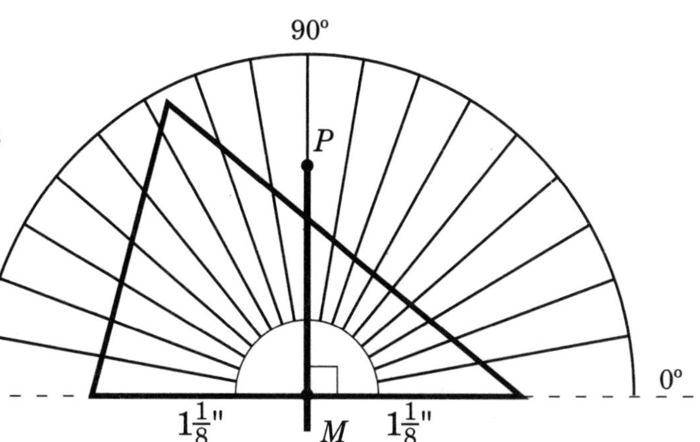

Practice

1. Draw the 3 medians of this triangle.

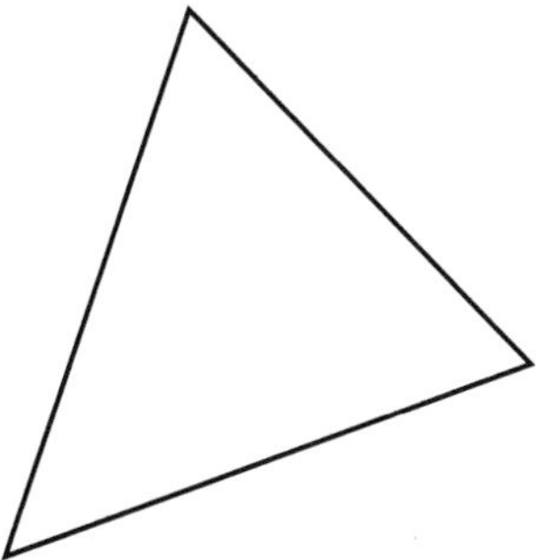

2. Draw the 3 altitudes of this triangle.

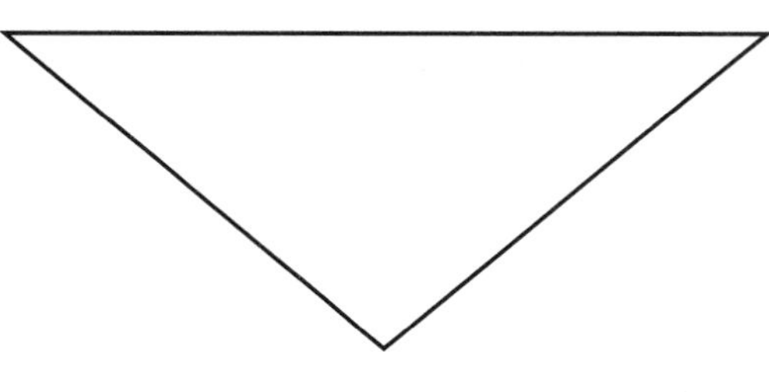

3. Draw the 3 perpendicular bisectors.

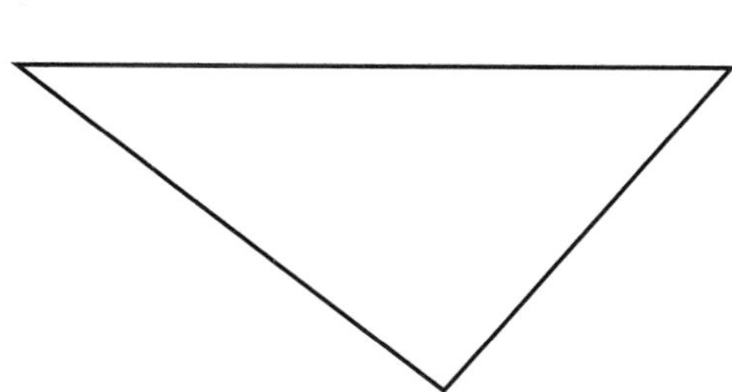

4. Draw the 3 midsegments of this triangle.

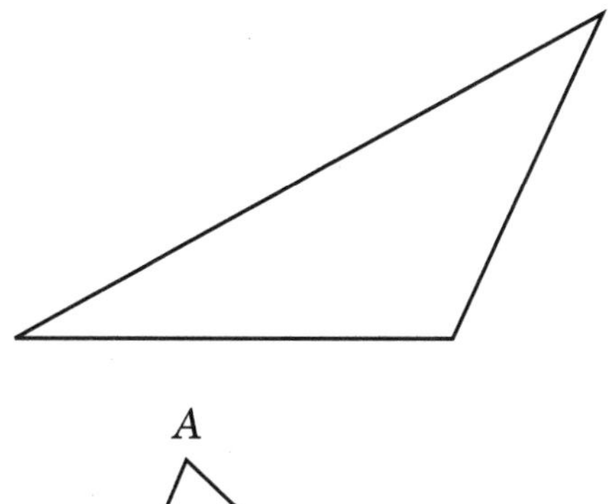

5. On this triangle, draw the median from A, the midsegment for sides $\overline{AB}$ and $\overline{BC}$, the altitude from A, and the perpendicular bisector of side $\overline{AC}$.

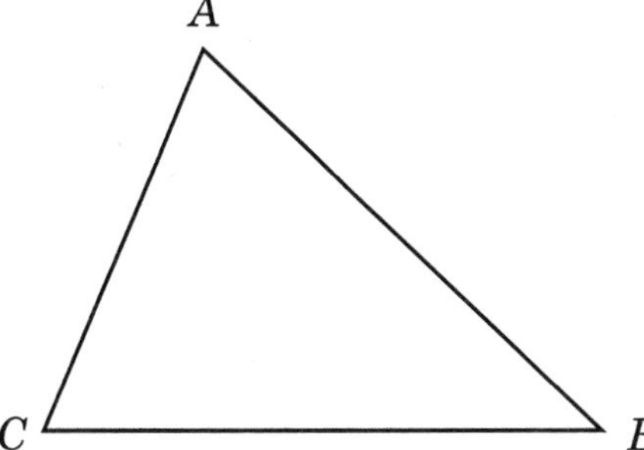

Chapter 5

More Special Segments

Isosceles Triangles

The altitude from the vertex angle of an isosceles triangle is also the median from the vertex angle, the bisector of the vertex angle, and the perpendicular bisector of the base.

Right Triangles

In a right triangle, the median from the right angle to the hypotenuse is equal in length to the two segments of the hypotenuse.

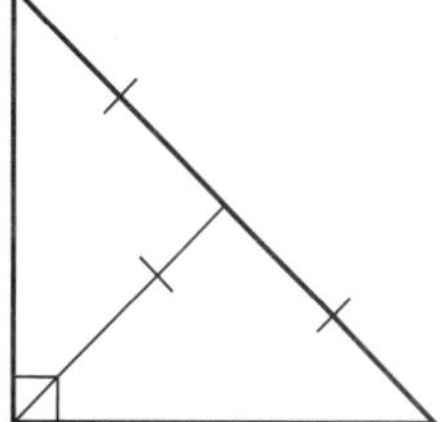

- In right triangle ΔABC,
  1. the length of altitude $\overline{BD}$ is equal to the geometric mean of AD and DC;
  2. the length of leg $\overline{BC}$ is equal to the geometric mean of CD and AC;
  3. the length of leg $\overline{BA}$ is equal to the geometric mean of AD and AC.
- The geometric mean of 2 numbers, a and b, is found by solving the proportion $\frac{a}{x} = \frac{x}{b}$, where value of x is the geometric mean of a and b. Applying the means-extreme property (cross-multiplication) shows that x^2 = ab. Taking the square root of both sides leads to $x = \sqrt{ab}$. So the geometric mean of a and b is $x = \sqrt{ab}$.

1. The length of the altitude to the hypotenuse of the right triangle ΔEFG can be found as follows:

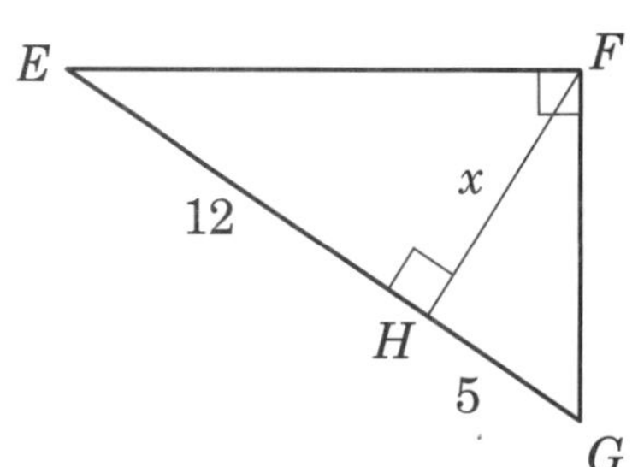

$$\frac{EH}{HF} = \frac{HF}{HG}$$
$$\frac{12}{x} = \frac{x}{5}$$
$$x^2 = 60$$
$$x = \sqrt{60}$$
$$x = 2\sqrt{15}$$

Therefore, $HF = 2\sqrt{15}$.

2. The length of the leg $\overline{RS}$ in right triangle ΔRST with altitude $\overline{US}$ can be found as follows:

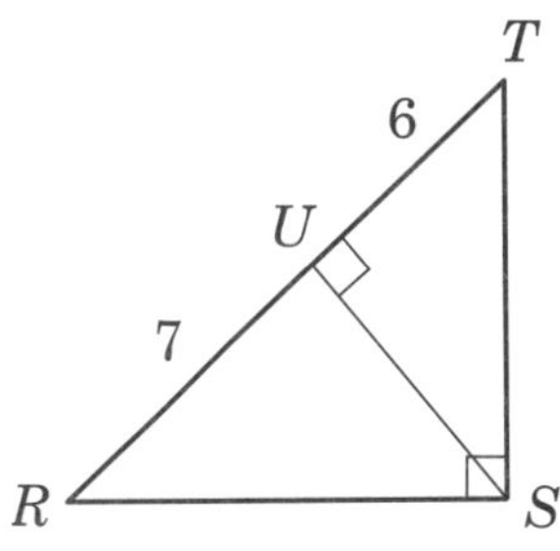

$$\frac{RU}{RS} = \frac{RS}{RT}$$
$$\frac{7}{x} = \frac{x}{13} \text{ (since } RT = RU + UT\text{)}$$
$$x^2 = 91$$
$$x = \sqrt{91}$$

Therefore, $RS = \sqrt{91}$.

3. If you know the length of altitude $\overline{MK}$ in right triangle ΔMNL and the length of one of the parts of the hypotenuse, you can find the length of the other part of the hpotenuse as follows:

$$\frac{KN}{MK} = \frac{MK}{KL}$$
$$\frac{4}{6} = \frac{6}{y}$$
$$4y = 36$$
$$y = 9$$

Therefore, $LK = 9$.

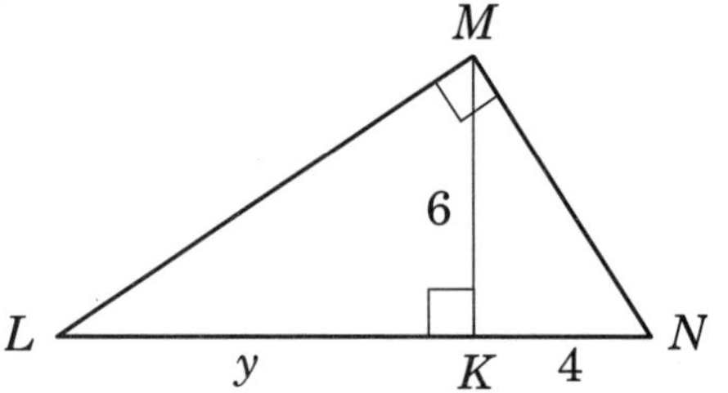

Midsegment

The midsegment is parallel to the third side and is half as long as the third side.

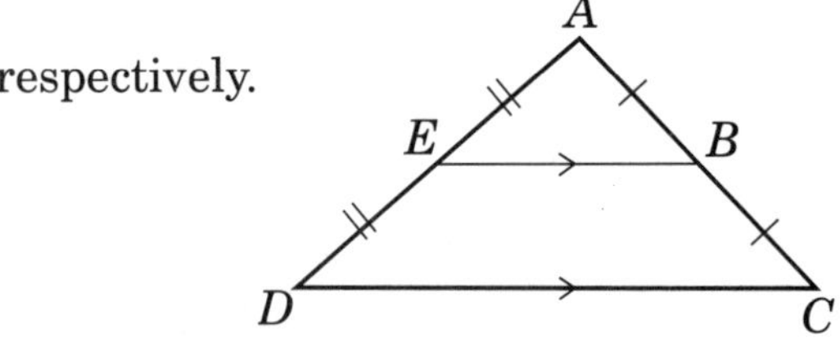

- In this case, E and B are midpoints of $\overline{AD}$ and $\overline{AC}$ respectively. Therefore, $\overline{EB} \parallel \overline{DC}$ and $EB = \frac{1}{2}DC$.

- In this case, since $\overline{VT}$ is parallel to $\overline{RS}$ and V is the midpoint of RU, $\overline{VT}$ is a midsegment. If we want to find the length of $\overline{VT}$, we need to remember that it is half the length of $\overline{RS}$.

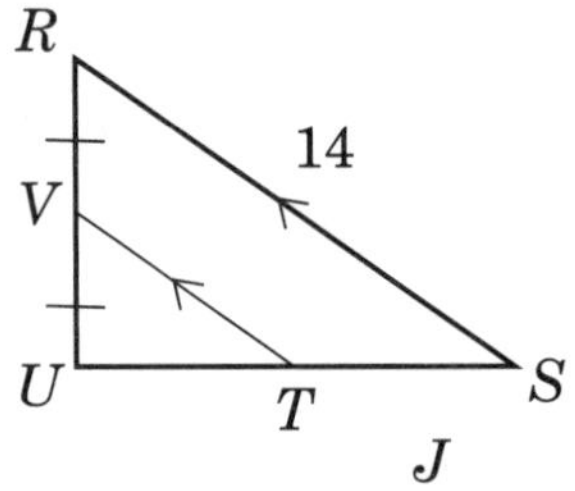

  $VT = \frac{1}{2}RS$

  $VT = \frac{1}{2}(14)$

  $VT = 7$

  The length of the midsegment is 7.

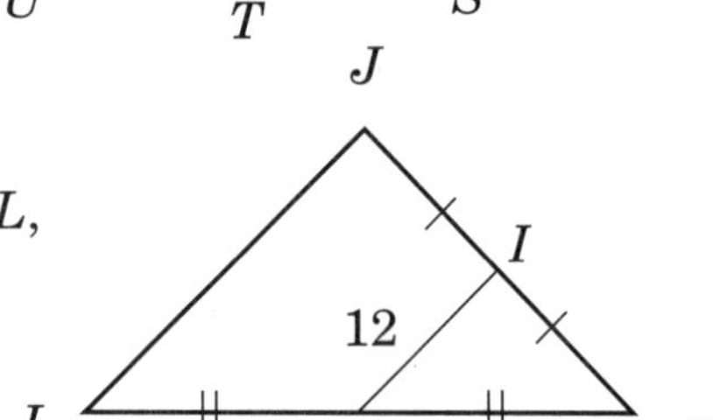

- And in this case, if I and H are midpoints in ΔJKL, then $HI = \frac{1}{2}LJ$. Since $HI = 12$, $12 = \frac{1}{2}LJ$, and $LJ = 24$.

Area

The altitude of a triangle is used as the height of that triangle when calculating area. The base, for use in the area formula, is the side to which the altitude is perpendicular.

Remember that the formula for the area of a triangle is $A = \frac{1}{2}bh$.

Practice

1.

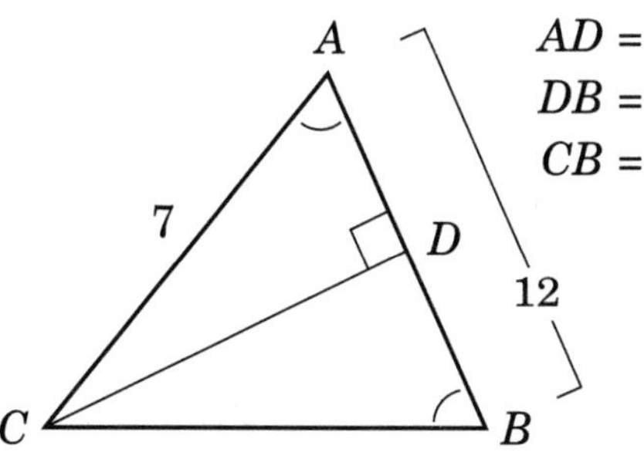

$AD =$
$DB =$
$CB =$

2. $\overline{YQ}$ is an altitude.

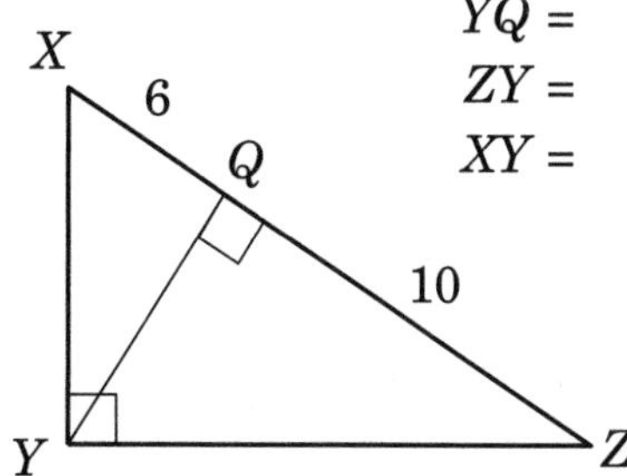

$YQ =$
$ZY =$
$XY =$

3.

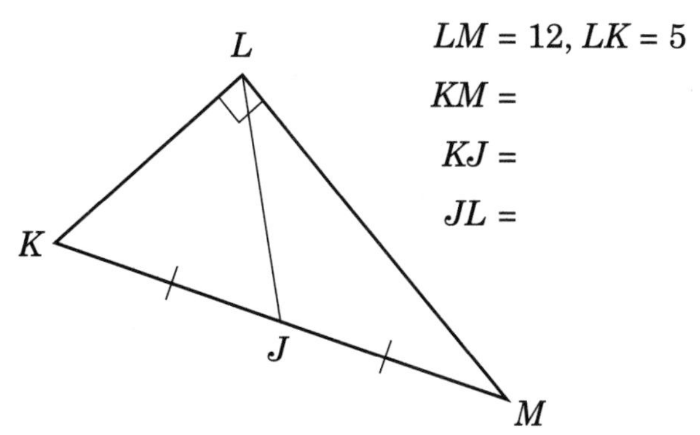

$LM = 12$, $LK = 5$
$KM =$
$KJ =$
$JL =$

4. $GH =$

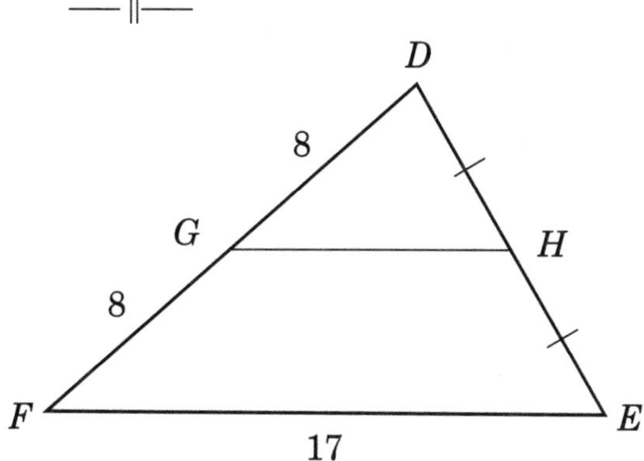

5. What is the area of ΔJKL if K and L are midpoints?

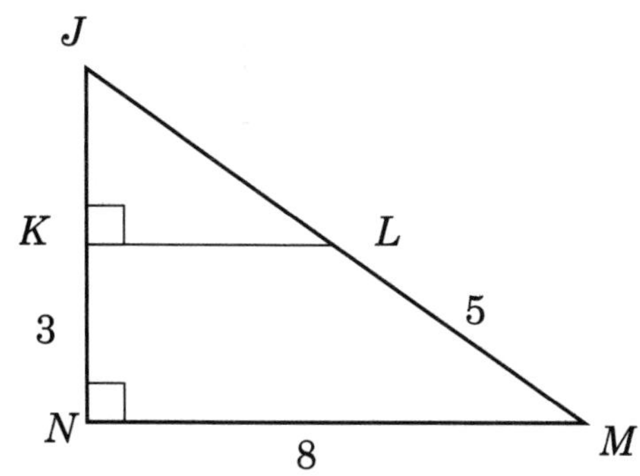

6. What is the $m\angle SUT$?
What is the $m\angle T$?
If $RT = 20$, what is the length of $\overline{US}$?

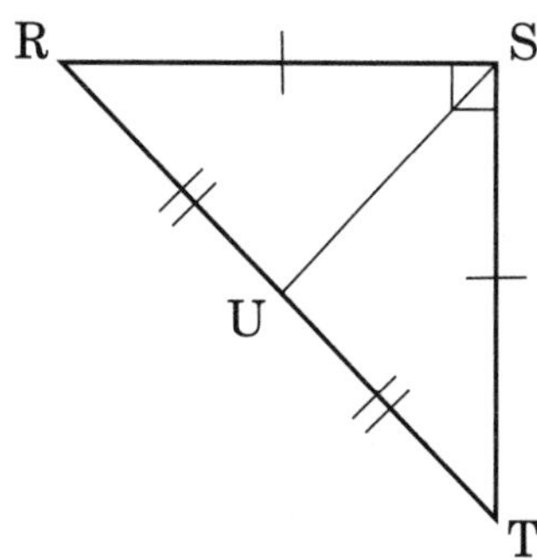

7. $NOPQ$ is a rectangle. $\overline{LK} \parallel \overline{ON}$
M is the midpoint of $\overline{OQ}$.

a. OQ = OM = MK =

b. What is the area of ΔOQN?

c. What is the area of rectangle $NOPQ$?

d. What is the area of ΔMQK?

e. What is the area of quadrilateral $OMKN$?

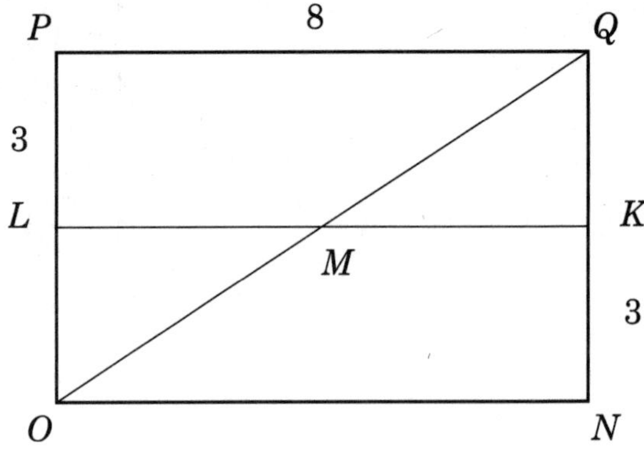

8. $ST = 15$, $PS = 10$, $PU = 5$, $RT = 6$.
$PQTS$ is a parallelogram.
V is the midpoint of $\overline{SQ}$.
The area of ΔSRQ is 84.

a. RQ =

b. What is the area of ΔSTQ?

c. UV =

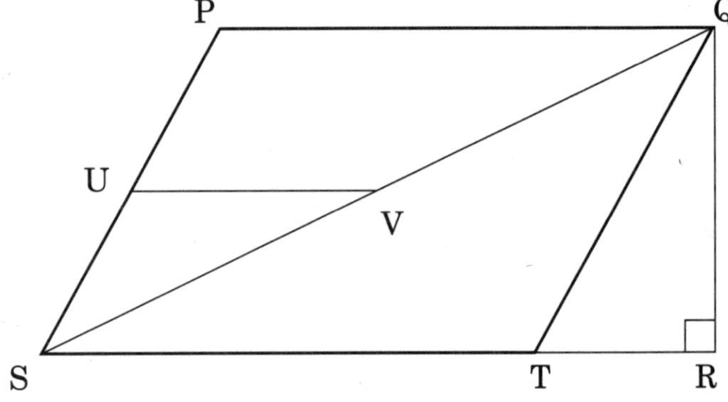

Chapter 6

Word Problems

Word Problem Examples

Problem: An obtuse isosceles triangle has sides that are 9", 9" and 16" long. Find the area of the triangle.

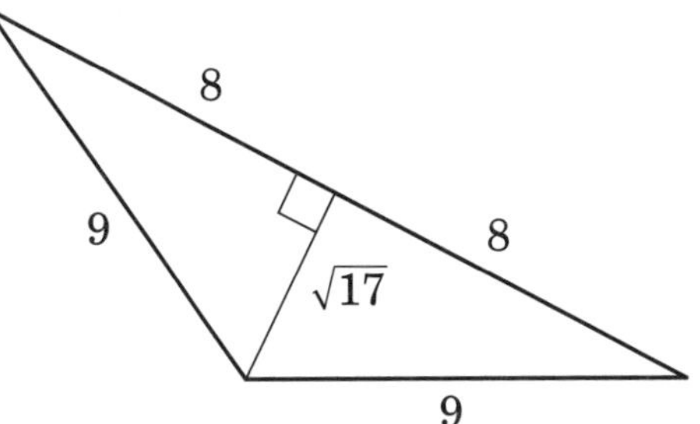

Answer: Since the altitude from the vertex angle of an isosceles triangle is also a median, the two pieces of the base are each $\frac{16}{2} = 8$ inches.

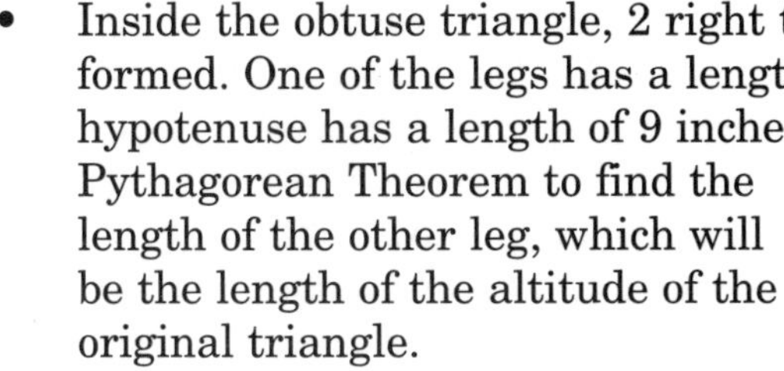

- Inside the obtuse triangle, 2 right triangles have been formed. One of the legs has a length of 8 inches and the hypotenuse has a length of 9 inches. We can use the Pythagorean Theorem to find the length of the other leg, which will be the length of the altitude of the original triangle.

$$a^2 + b^2 = c^2$$
$$8^2 + b^2 = 9^2$$
$$64 + b^2 = 81$$
$$b^2 = 17$$
$$b = \sqrt{17}$$

- Since the altitude of a triangle is also its height, we now know the base and height of this triangle: b = 16 inches and $h = \sqrt{17}$. The formula for finding the area of a triangle is $A = \frac{1}{2}bh$, so: $A = \frac{1}{2}(16)(\sqrt{17})$

  $A = 8\sqrt{17}$

  Therefore the area of this triangle is $8\sqrt{17}$ in^2.

14m
50m
48m

Problem: Your neighbor has an oddly shaped front yard and is having trouble determining its area. In order to buy the right amount of weed killer, she needs to know this area and asks for your help. The yard is shaped like a right triangle and has sides of length 14 meters, 48 meters, and 50 meters. If 1 bottle of weed killer will cover 40m^2 of lawn, how many bottles does she need to buy?

Answer: When we have a right triangle, the base is one of the legs and the height is the other leg for the purpose of finding the area. We need to realize that since the hypotenuse of a right triangle is always the longest side, the 50 meter side must be the hypotenuse. So we can pick 14 meters as our base and 48 meters as our height.

$$A = \tfrac{1}{2}bh$$
$$A = \tfrac{1}{2}(14)(48)$$
$$A = 336\text{m}^2$$

- Now that we know the area of your neighbor's yard, we need to figure out how many bottles of weed killer to buy. Since she can cover 40m^2 with 1 bottle, we need to divide the area of her yard by the amount 1 bottle will cover.

  $\frac{336m^2}{40m^2} = 8.4$ But we know that she can't buy $\frac{4}{10}$ of a bottle, so she'll have to buy 9 bottles and then she'll have some left over.

Practice

1. What is the area of a 30–60–90 triangle whose longest leg has a length of $4\sqrt{3}$?
2. An isosceles triangle has sides that are 5cm, 5cm and 9cm. What is the area of this triangle?
3. A square has a diagonal length of 24 inches. What is its area?
4. One of the base angles of an isosceles trangle has a measure of 30 degrees. If one of the legs of the isosceles triangle is 8 centimeters, find the area of the triangle.
5. The wall along your stairway needs to be repainted and you are trying to decide how much paint to buy. Each step is 9 inches tall and 12 inches deep. The wall extends 8 feet above the top step and the wall stops with perpendicular lines through A and B. If a gallon of paint will cover 150 ft^2, how many gallons will you need?

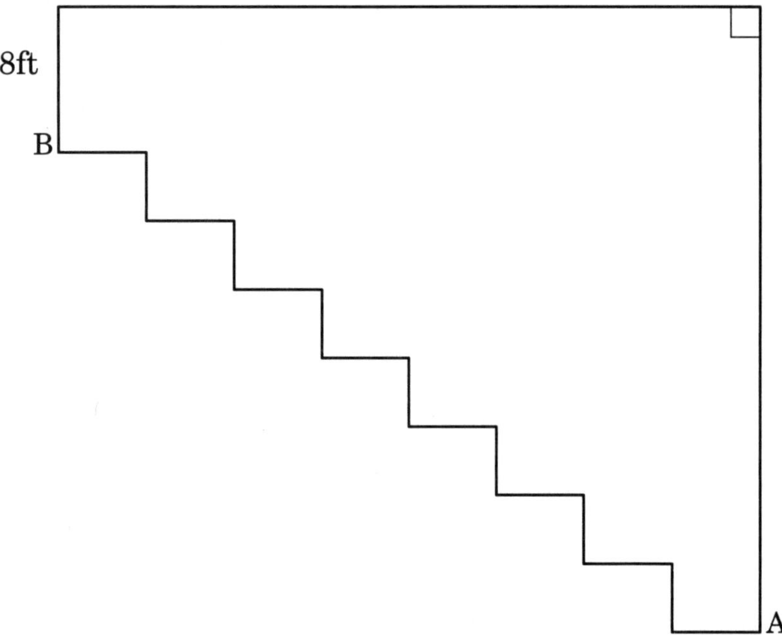

Chapter 7

Congruent Triangles

Defining Congruent Triangles

Two triangles are congruent if they have the same size and shape. This means that their corresponding sides and corresponding angles will be congruent.

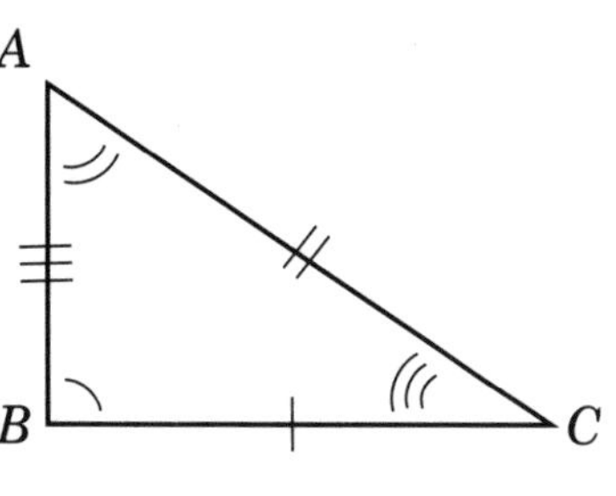

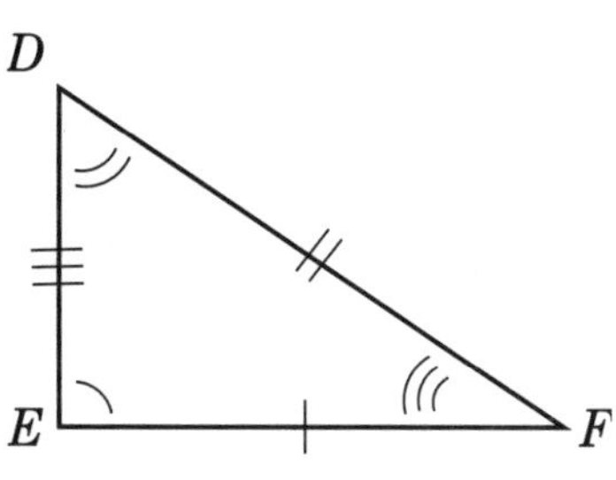

- $\Delta CAB \cong \Delta FDE$
  - The sides of ΔABC are congruent to the corresponding sides of ΔDEF.
    $\overline{AB} \cong \overline{DE}$ $\overline{BC} \cong \overline{EF}$ $\overline{AC} \cong \overline{DF}$
  - The angles of ΔABC are congruent to the corresponding angles of ΔDEF.
    $\angle A \cong \angle D$ $\angle B \cong \angle E$ $\angle C \cong \angle F$

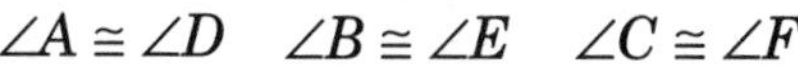

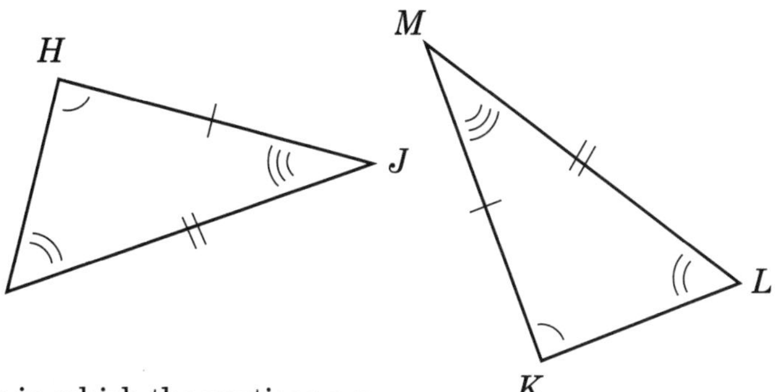

- Triangles do not have to be facing the same direction to be congruent.

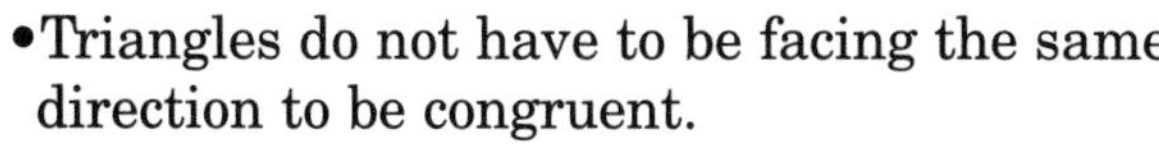

- $\Delta JHI \cong \Delta MKL$. The corresponding parts are shown to be congruent in the illustration.

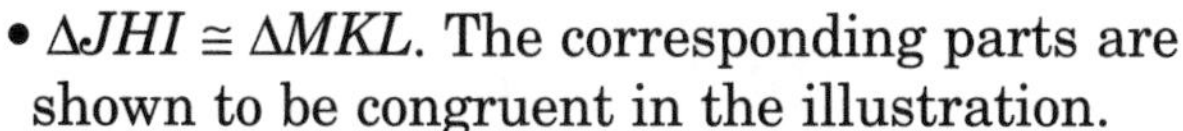

- Parts are corresponding when they are in the same relative position. If you were to lay the two triangles on top of each other, their corresponding parts would line up.
- When naming two congruent triangles, the order in which the vertices are named is important. The first triangle can be named in any way. The second triangle in the congruency statement must be named so that the corresponding vertices are listed in the same order as the first triangle.

Practice

Write a congruency statement and list the corresponding parts for each pair of triangles.

Example

Congruency Statement: $\Delta XYZ \cong \Delta RQV$

Corresponding Parts: $\overline{XY} \cong \overline{RQ}, \overline{YZ} \cong \overline{QV}$

$\overline{XZ} \cong \overline{RV}$, $\angle X \cong \angle R$, $\angle Y \cong \angle Q$, $\angle Z \cong \angle V$

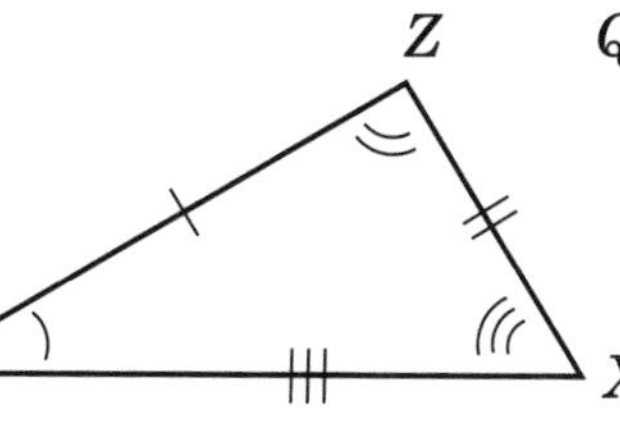

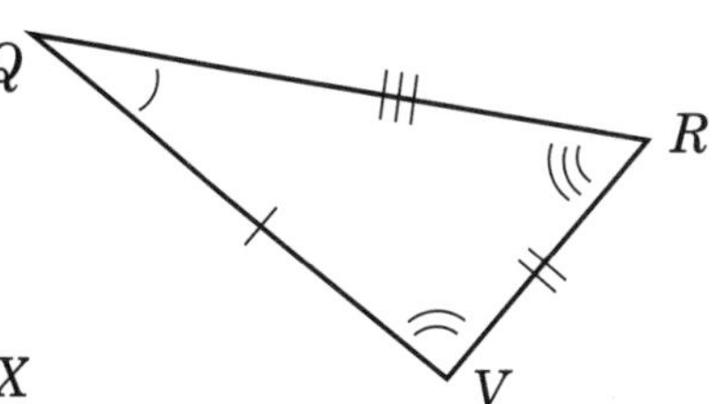

1.

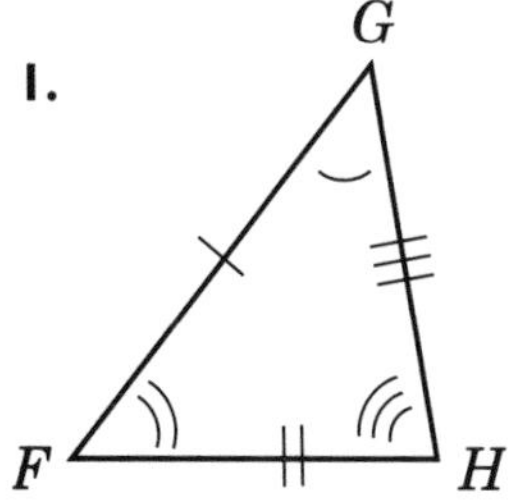

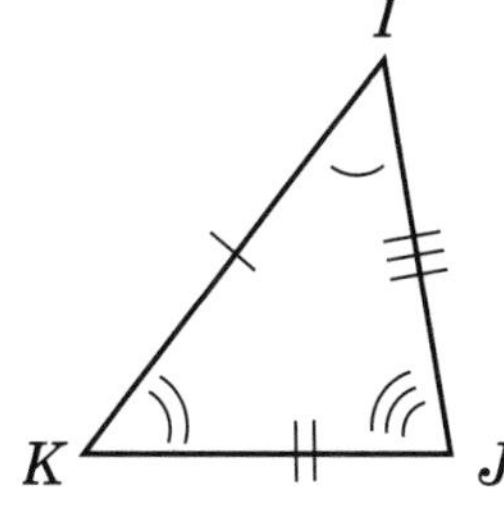

2.

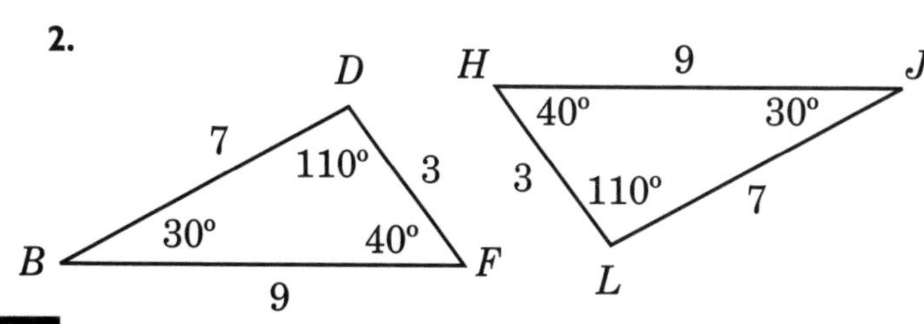

Finding Unknown Measures

If you know that two triangles are congruent, you can use information about one triangle to determine the measurements of the other triangle.

- $\triangle RAF \cong \triangle SYQ$

  Since we know that these are congruent triangles, we know that their corresponding parts are congruent.

  $m\angle R = 30°$, so $m\angle S = 30°$

  $m\angle Y = 130°$, so $m\angle A = 130°$

  $AF = 8$, so $YQ = 8$

  $SY = 3$, so $RA = 3$

  $QS = 10$, so $FR = 10$

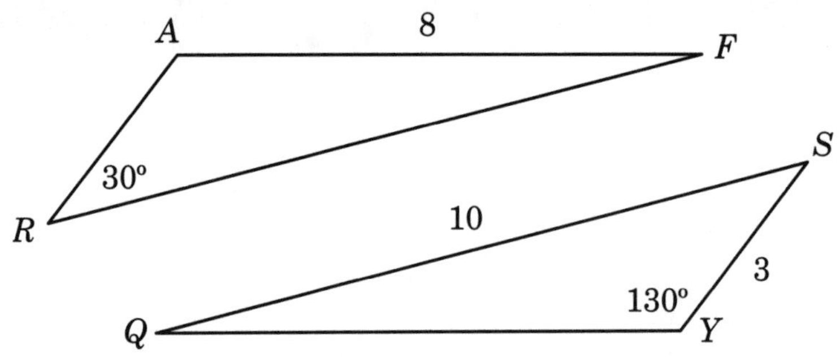

- Since the sum of the interior angles of a triangle is 180°, and since we know that two of the angles in these triangles are 30° and 130°, $m\angle F = m\angle Q = 180° - (130° + 30°) = 20°$.

Practice

Find the missing measurements in each of these pairs of congruent triangles.

1. $\triangle KET \cong \triangle YCO$

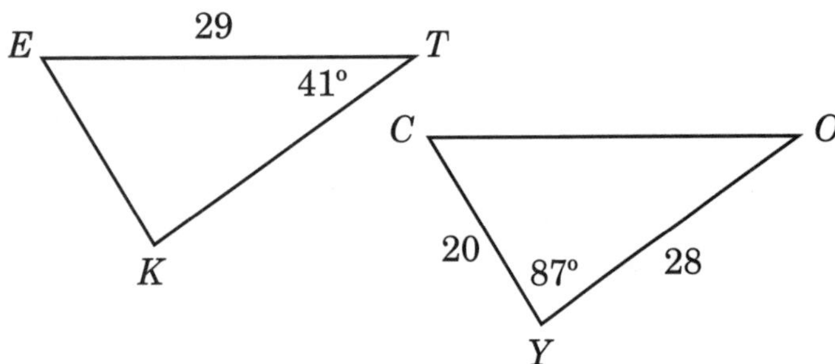

2.  $\triangle WMI \cong \triangle QLS$

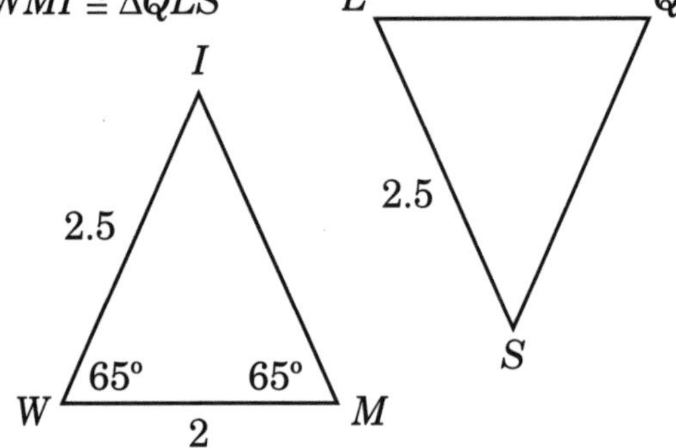

3.  $\triangle CNZ \cong \triangle BRZ$

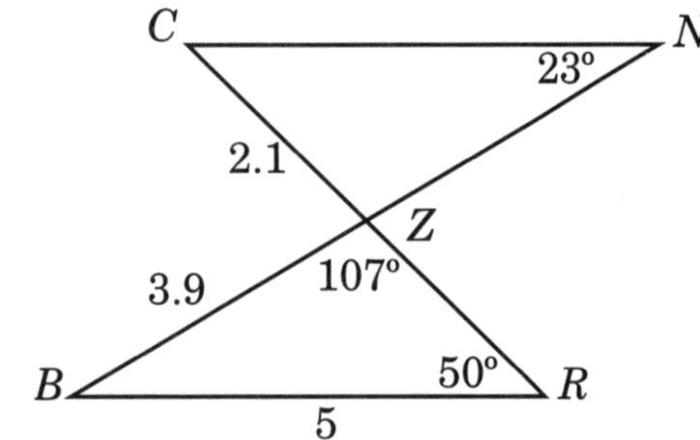

4. $\triangle DAH \cong \triangle XHA$

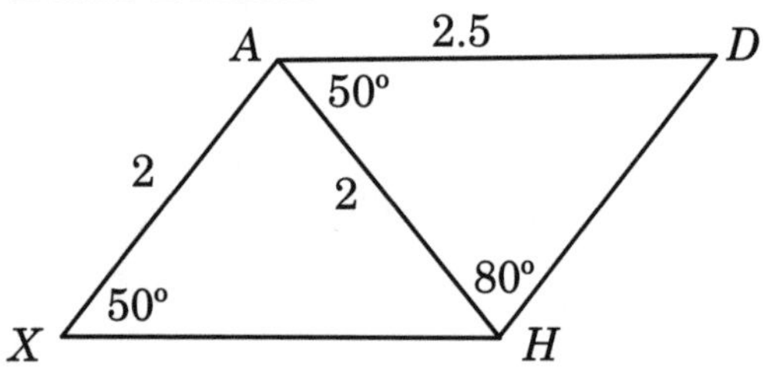

5. $\triangle VUI \cong \triangle KUI$

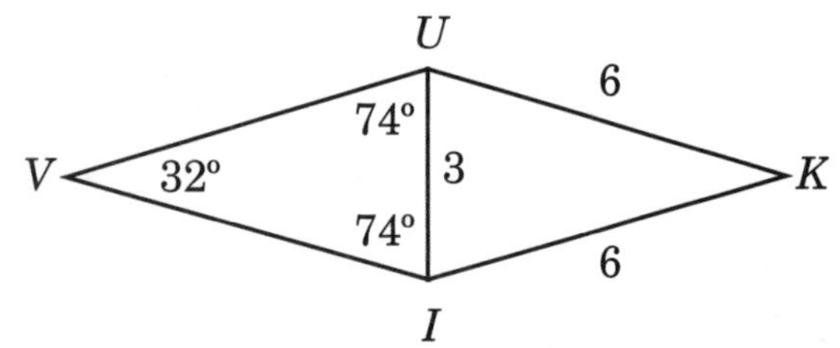

6. 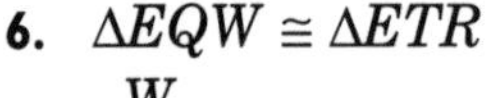 $\triangle EQW \cong \triangle ETR$

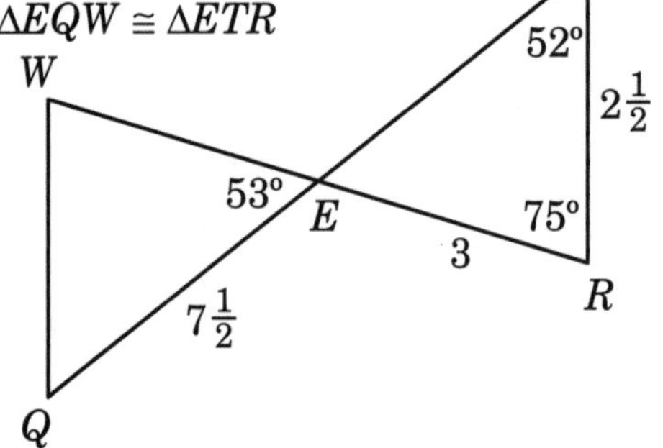

Proving Triangles Congruent 1

Information that can be used to prove that two triangles are congruent:

- **SSS or Side-Side-Side:** Two triangles are congruent if all 3 pairs of corresponding sides are congruent.
- **SAS or Side-Angle-Side:** Two triangles are congruent if two pairs of corresponding sides are congruent and the corresponding angles between the sides are congruent.
- **ASA or Angle-Side-Angle:** Two triangles are congruent if two pairs of corresponding angles are congruent and the corresponding sides between the angles are congruent.
- **AAS or Angle-Angle-Side:** Two triangles are congruent if two pairs of corresponding angles are congruent and a pair of corresponding sides that is not between the angles are congruent.
- **HL or Hypotenuse-Leg**: Two right triangles are congruent if they have a pair of congruent legs and their hypotenuses are congruent.

Examples of SSS, SAS, ASA, AAS, and HL

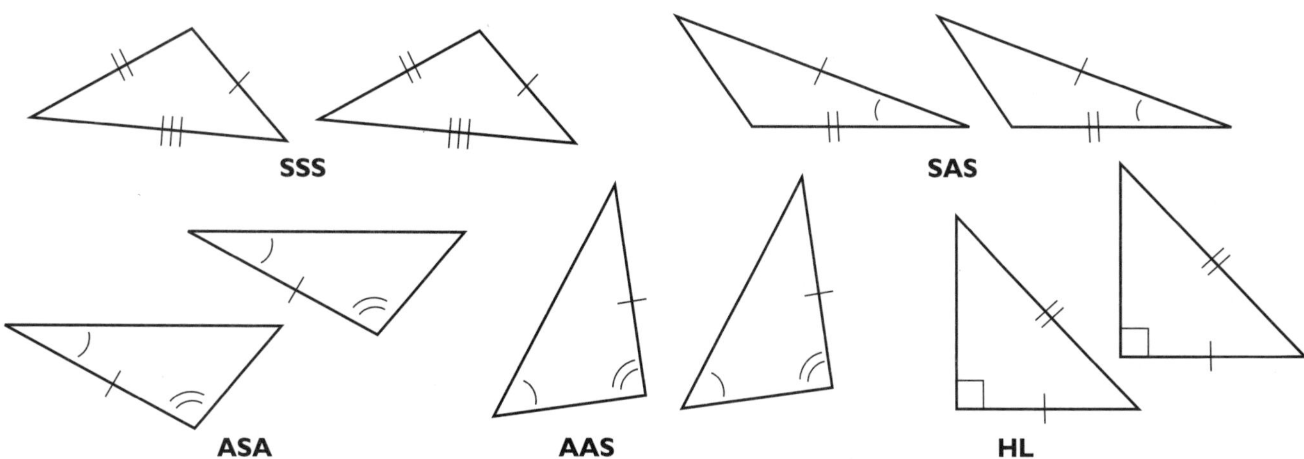

Examples that often cause confusion:

- This is not SAS because the corresponding congruent angles are not between the congruent sides.

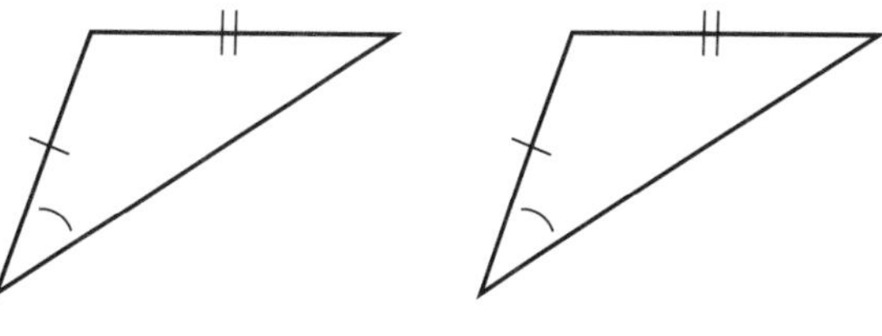

- This is not ASA because the congruent sides are not between the congruent angles. It is not AAS because the congruent sides do not correspond (they come from different angles).

- This is not HL because the hypotenuse is not one of the congruent sides. It is SAS, however, because the angle between the congruent corresponding sides is a right angle, and therefore congruent from one triangle to the other.

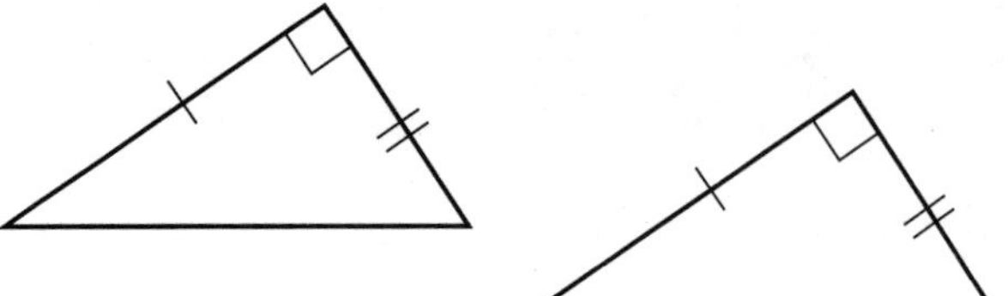

Practice

State which method can be used to prove that the triangles are congruent, or state that they are not congruent. If they are congruent, write a congruency statement.

1.

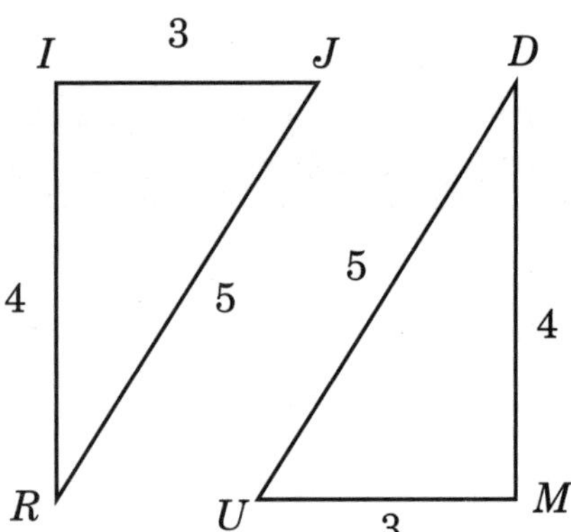

2.

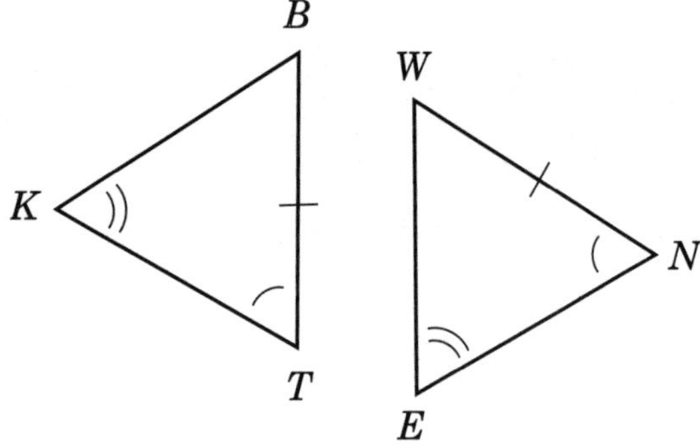

3.

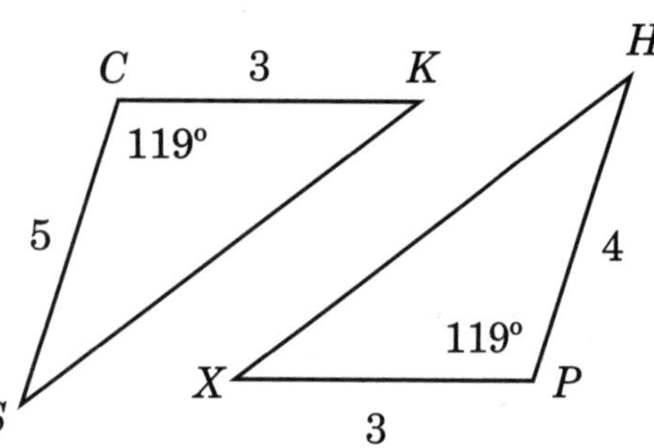

4.

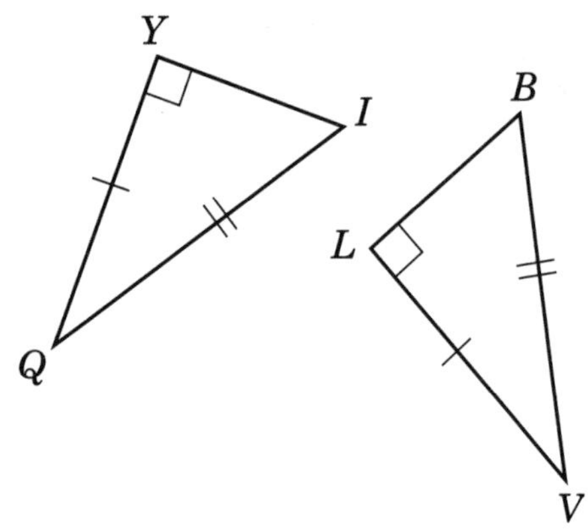

5.

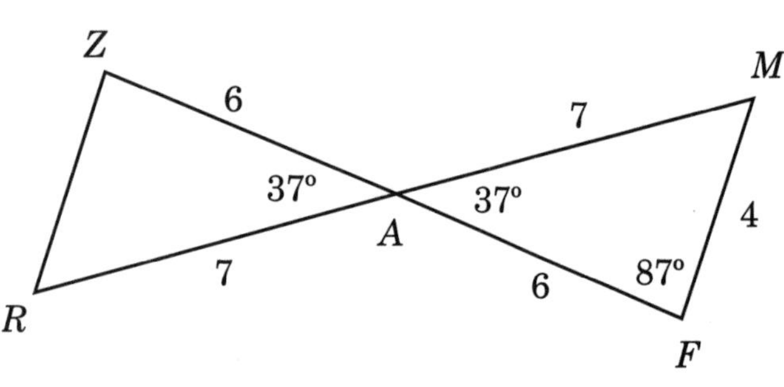

6.

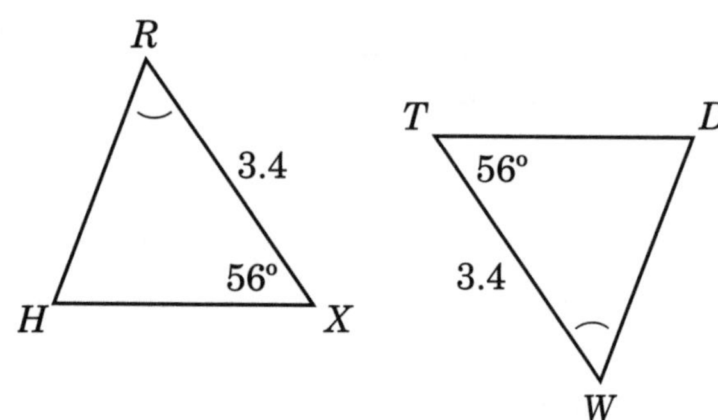

7.

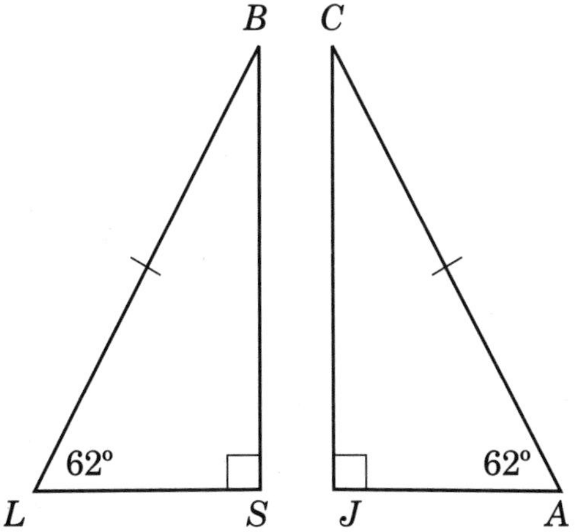

8.

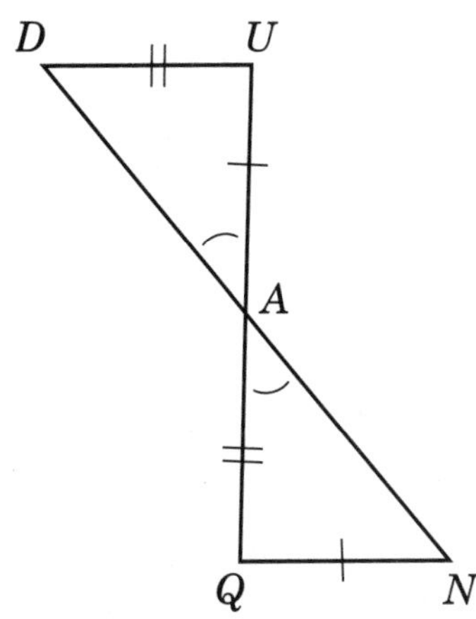

Proving Triangles Congruent 2

Sometimes you must determine which parts of the triangles are congruent based on other information in the picture before you can determine if the triangles are congruent.

- There are three different ways to show that $\Delta BAC \cong \Delta DCA$.
    1. **SSS:** Opposite sides of a parallelogram are congruent, $\overline{AD} \cong \overline{BC}$ and $\overline{AB} \cong \overline{DC}$. The two triangles share the diagonal, $\overline{AC}$, so that acts as a pair of congruent sides as well.

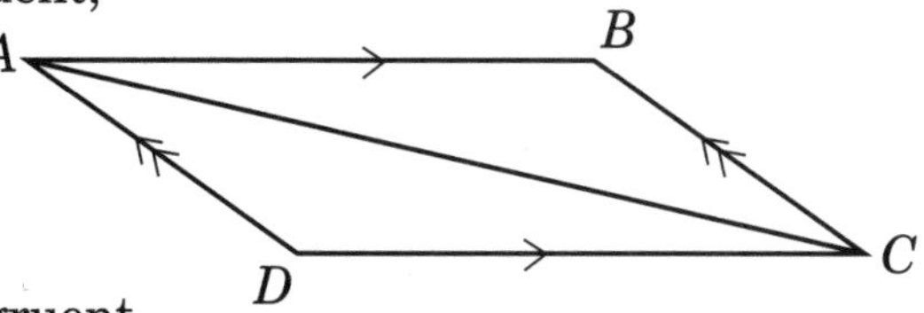

    2. **SAS:** In a parallelogram, opposite angles are congruent. Therefore, $\angle D \cong \angle B$. In #1 it was explained that $\overline{AD} \cong \overline{BC}$ and $\overline{AB} \cong \overline{DC}$.
    3. **ASA:** Since $\overline{AC}$ is a transversal cutting two different pairs of parallel lines, it creates two sets of congruent alternate interior angles: $\angle DAC \cong \angle BCA$ and $\angle BAC \cong \angle DCA$. With all angles known to be congruent, you can pick which side from the explanation in #1 to complete the information.

- There are two different ways to show that $\Delta RQS \cong \Delta TUS$.
    1. **AAS:** $\angle QRS \cong \angle STU$ and $\angle RQS \cong \angle TUS$ because they are alternate interior angles. $\overline{TS}$ is shown to be congruent to $\overline{SR}$.
    2. **ASA:** $\angle QRS \cong \angle UST$ because they are vertical angles. $\angle QRS \cong \angle STU$ because they are alternate interior angles. $\overline{TS}$ is shown to be congruent to $\overline{SR}$.

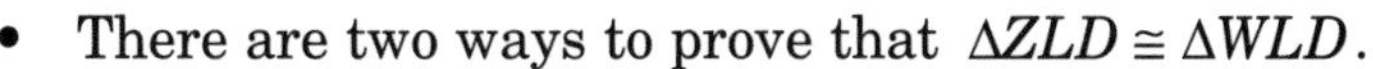

- There are two ways to prove that $\Delta ZLD \cong \Delta WLD$.
    1. **ASA:** ΔZLW is an isosceles triangle, so its base angles are congruent. $\overline{WL} \cong \overline{ZL}$ (and $\angle DLW \cong \angle DLZ$ according to the picture).
    2. **SAS:** The two triangles share $\overline{DL}$. $\angle DLW \cong \angle DLZ$ (and $\overline{WL} \cong \overline{ZL}$ according to the picture).

Practice

Explain whether or not each pair of triangles is congruent. Provide the method and write a congruency statement if they are congruent.

1. N is the midpoint of $\overline{AH}$.

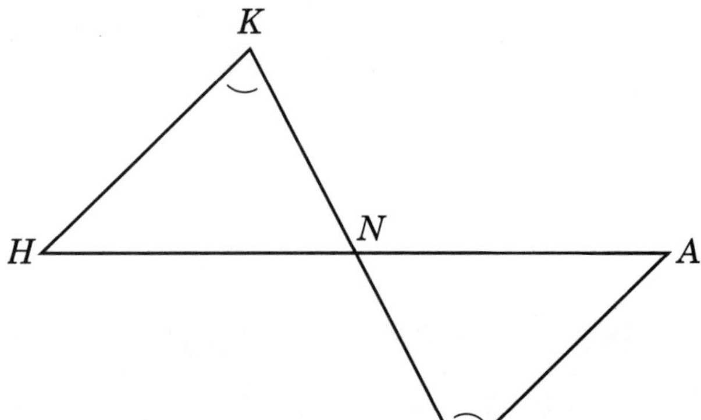

2. $FNVL$ is a rectangle.

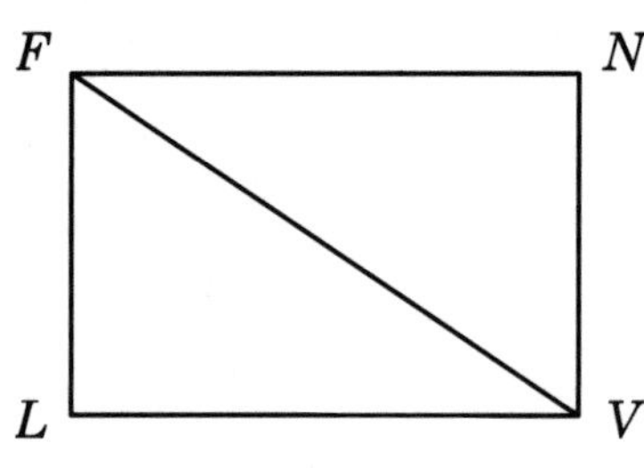

3.

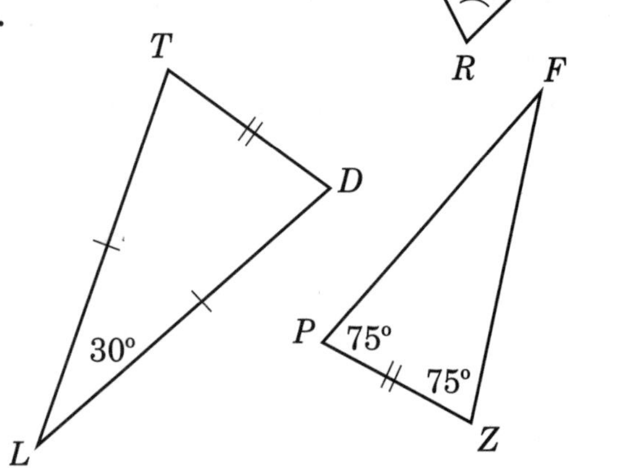

4.

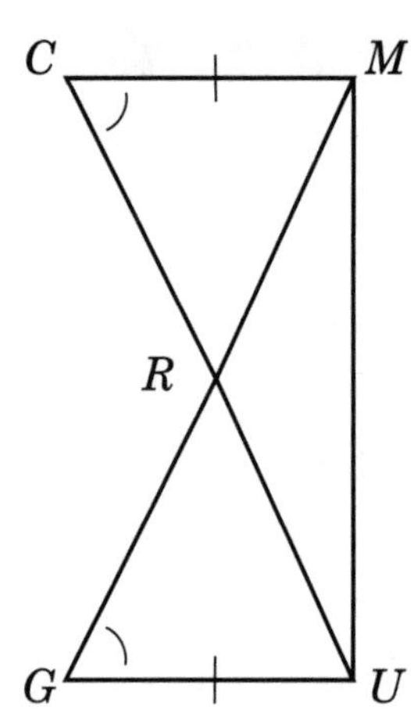

5.

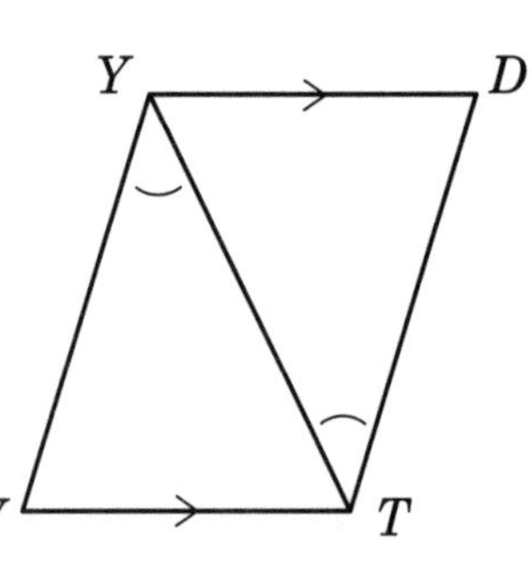

6.

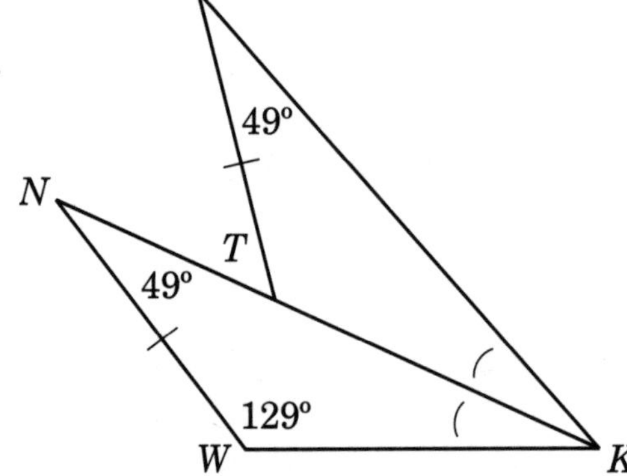

7.

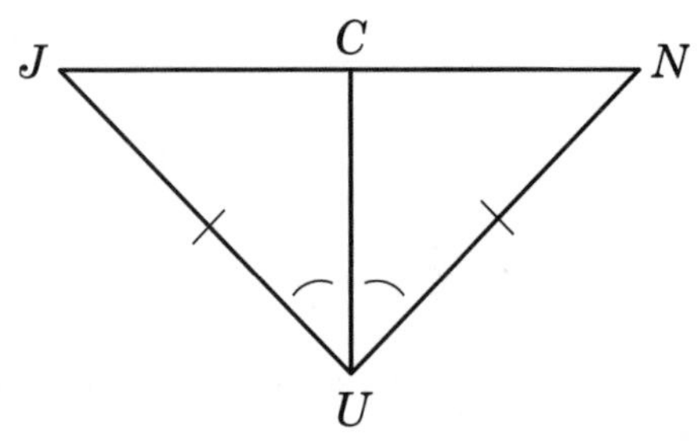

8. $EIOD$ is a square.
$EKVI$ is an isosceles trapezoid.

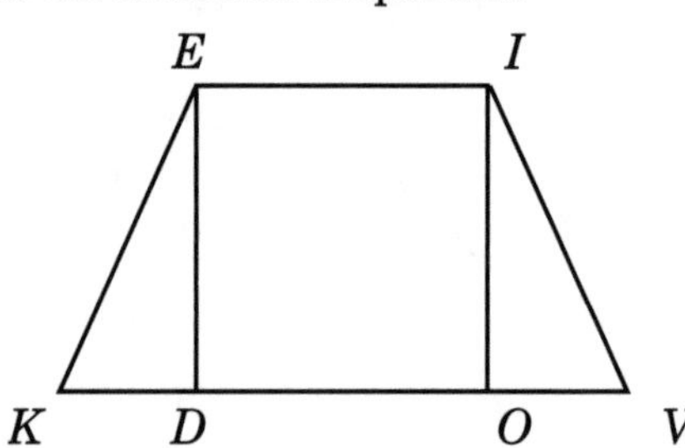

Chapter 8

Similar Triangles

What Makes Triangles Similar?

Two triangles are similar if their corresponding angles are congruent and their sides are in proportion. When two triangles are similar, they look exactly the same, except one looks as though it was enlarged in a photocopier. The symbol for "is similar to" is ~.

$\Delta ABC \sim \Delta EFG$

- *Corresponding angles are congruent.*

  This is like in congruent triangles.

  $\angle A \cong \angle E \quad \angle B \cong \angle F \quad \angle C \cong \angle G$

- *Sides are in proportion.*

  When sides are in proportion, the ratio of a side of one triangle to the corresponding side of the other triangle is consistent. $\frac{AB}{EF} = \frac{BC}{FG} = \frac{AC}{EG}$

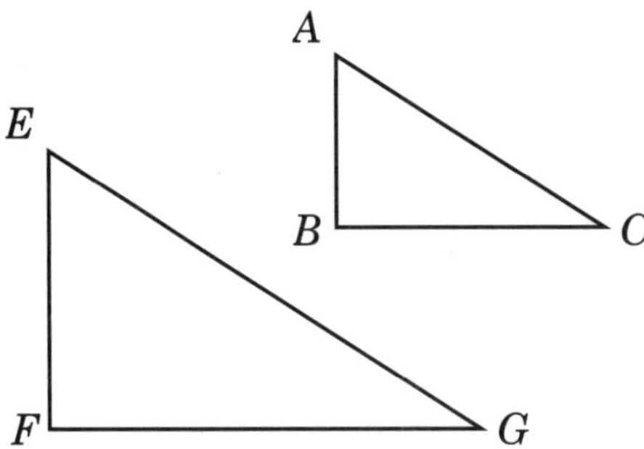

- *Scale factor*

  The scale factor is the simplified form of the ratios expressed above. It is used to find the unknown lengths of sides in either of the similar triangles in the pair.

If it is given that $\Delta HIJ \sim \Delta KLM$ *. . .*

- *corresponding angles are congruent*

  $m\angle H = 110°$, so $m\angle K = 110°$

  $m\angle M = 43°$, so $m\angle J = 43°$

  $m\angle H + m\angle J = 110° + 43° = 153°$

  $m\angle I = 180° - 153° = 27°$, so $m\angle L = 27°$

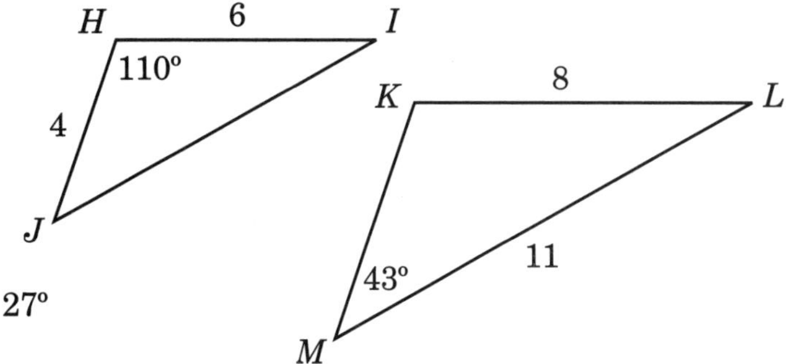

- *corresponding sides are in proportion*

  - $\overline{HI}$ and $\overline{KL}$ are corresponding sides for which measures are given on both triangles. Therefore, you can use them to calculate the scale factor.

    $\frac{HI}{KL} = \frac{6}{8} = \frac{3}{4}$ The scale factor for the small triangle to the large triangle is 3:4.

    Once you have found the scale factor, you must make all further calculations by comparing the triangles in the same order – in this case, small to large.

    You can then use the scale factor to find the other measures.

    $\frac{3}{4} = \frac{HJ}{KM}$ because $\overline{HJ}$ and $\overline{KM}$ are corresponding sides.

    $\frac{3}{4} = \frac{4}{KM}$ using cross-multiplication $3KM = 16$ and $KM = \frac{16}{3}$ or $KM = 5\frac{2}{3}$.

    $\frac{3}{4} = \frac{JI}{ML}$ because $\overline{JI}$ and $\overline{ML}$ are corresponding sides.

    $\frac{3}{4} = \frac{JI}{11}$ $33 = 4JI$ and $JI = \frac{33}{4}$ or $JI = 8\frac{1}{4}$.

If it is given that $\Delta ZYX \sim \Delta WVU$, *then*

- *corresponding angles are congruent,* so:

  $m\angle Z = 64° = m\angle W$

  $m\angle X = 33° = m\angle U$

  $m\angle Z + m\angle X = 64° + 33° = 97°$

  $m\angle Y = m\angle V = 180° - 97° = 83°$

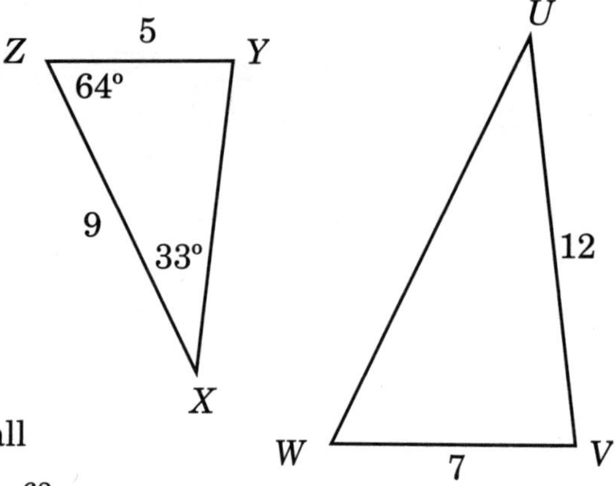

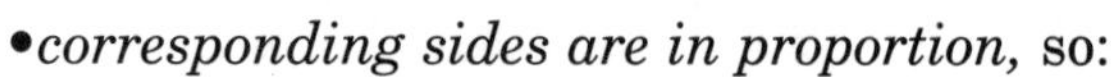

- *corresponding sides are in proportion,* so:
  - *scale factor*

  $\frac{WV}{ZY} = \frac{7}{5}$ if we compare the large triangle to the small

  $\frac{7}{5} = \frac{UW}{ZX}$ so $\frac{7}{5} = \frac{UW}{9}$ and $63 = 5UW$, therefore $UW = \frac{63}{5} = 12.6$

  $\frac{7}{5} = \frac{UV}{XY}$ so $\frac{7}{5} = \frac{12}{XY}$ and $60 = 7XY$, therefore $XY = \frac{60}{7} \approx 8.6$

Practice

For each pair of similar triangles: a.) Find the missing angle measures, b.) Calculate the scale factor, and c.) Find the missing lengths of sides.

1. $\Delta JKL \sim \Delta NOM$

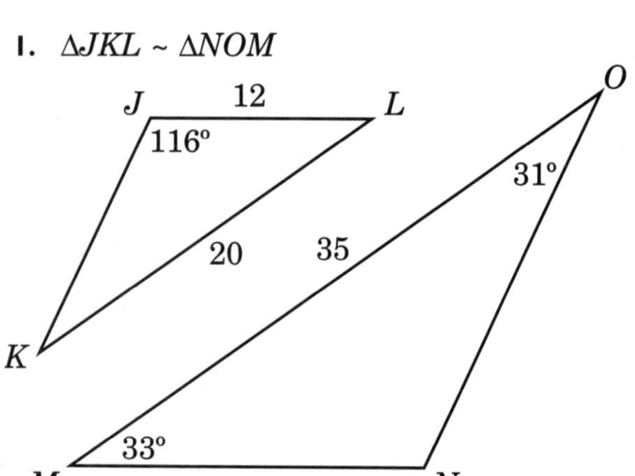

2. $\Delta ACD \sim \Delta GCI$

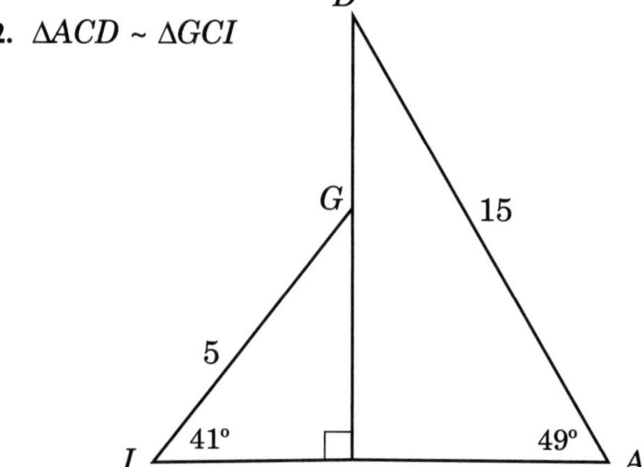

3. $\Delta RSU \sim \Delta SUT$

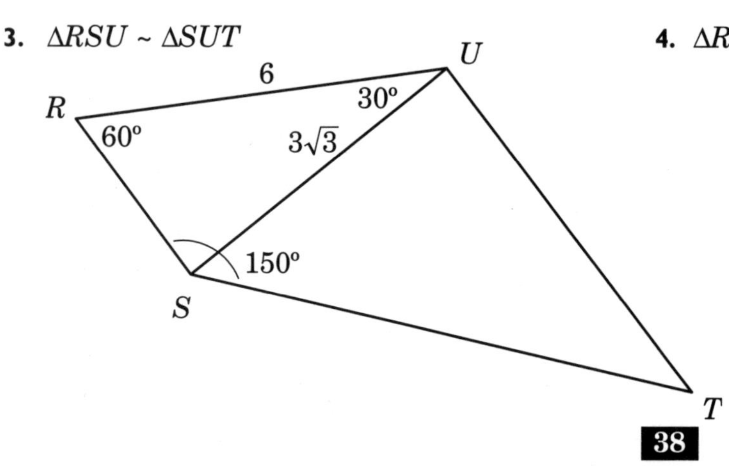

4. $\Delta RHL \sim \Delta MGI$

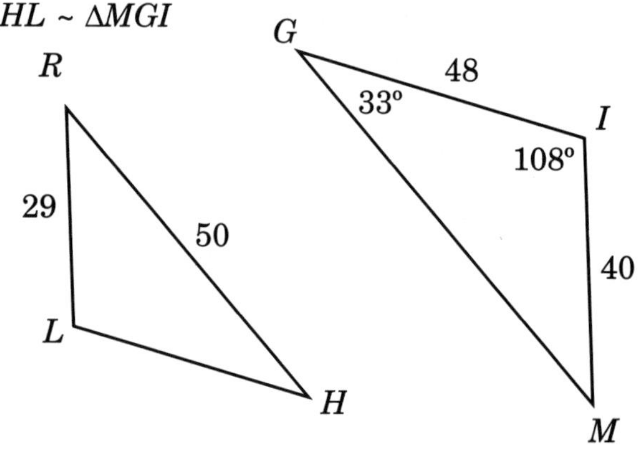

Proving Triangles Similar

Just as there are ways to prove that two triangles are congruent, there are also ways to prove that two triangles are similar. Each of the methods relies on the two aspects of similarity: the corresponding angles are congruent and the corresponding sides are in proportion.

- There are three sets of information for proving that two triangles are similar:
  - **AA ~ or Angle-Angle Similarity Postulate:** Two triangles are similar if two pairs of corresponding angles are congruent. Keep in mind that if two pairs of angles are congruent, then the third pair is also congruent.
  - **SAS ~ or Side-Angle-Side Similarity Theorem:** Two triangles are similar if two pairs of corresponding sides are in proportion (the ratios for each pair are the same when reduced) and the corresponding angles between them are congruent.
  - **SSS ~ or Side-Side-Side Similarity Theorem:** Two triangles are similar if all three pairs of corresponding sides are in proportion (all three pairs are in the same ratio when reduced).

Examples of AA~, SAS~ and SSS~

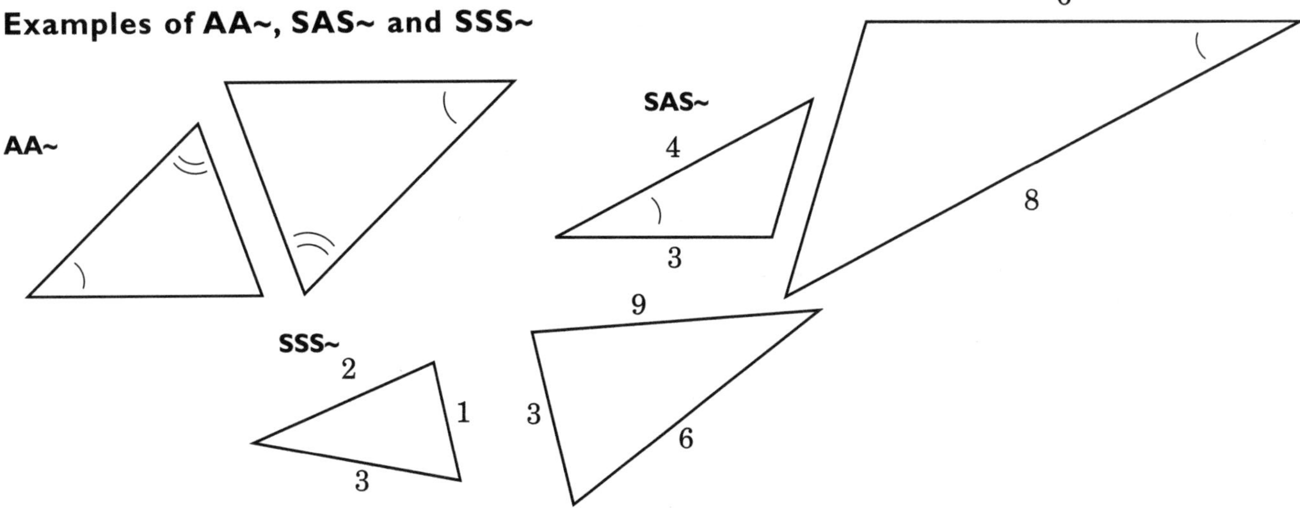

In order to apply AA~, SAS~ or SSS~ and to state that two triangles are similar, it is necessary to test the given information to ensure that the measurements meet the requirements, and not just that the information is given in the right places.

- ΔABC appears to be similar to ΔDEF by SAS~. To determine if this is the case, we must check to see if the given information fits the requirement. They will be similar if and only if $\frac{AC}{DF} = \frac{AB}{DE}$ and if $m\angle A = m\angle D$.
  - $\frac{AC}{DF} = \frac{2}{4} = \frac{1}{2}$ and $\frac{AB}{DE} = \frac{1.5}{3} = \frac{1}{2}$, so the sides are in proportion.
  - $m\angle F + m\angle E = 45° + 70° = 115°$, so $m\angle D = 180° - 115° = 65°$. Since $m\angle A = 65°$, $m\angle A = m\angle D$.
  - Both parts of the requirements for SAS~ are met, so $\Delta ABC \sim \Delta DEF$.

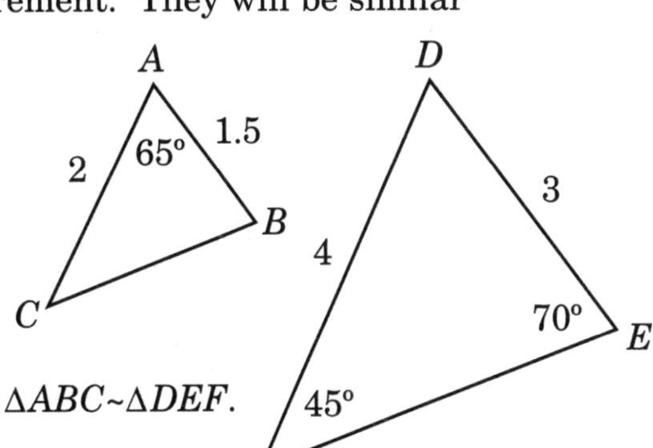

• ΔXYZ appears to be similar to ΔLMN *by* SSS~. If they are, then the 3 pairs of corresponding sides have to be in proportion.

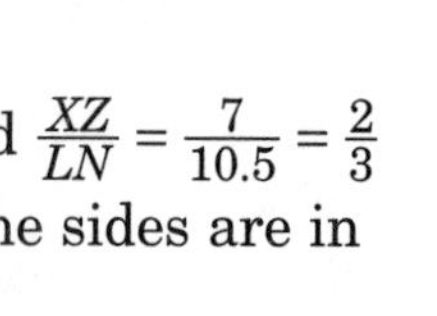

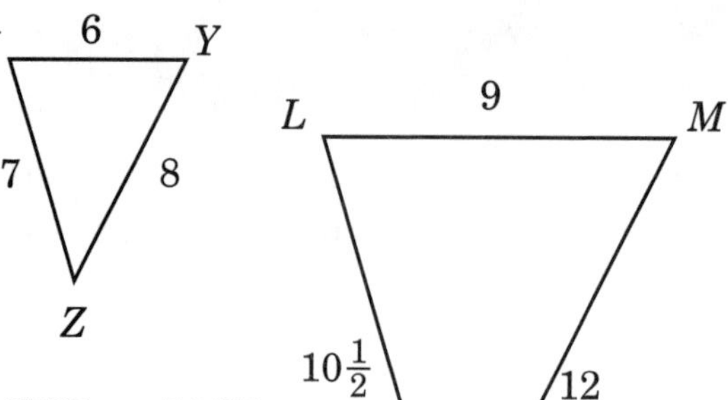

- $\frac{XY}{LM} = \frac{6}{9} = \frac{2}{3}$ and $\frac{YZ}{MN} = \frac{8}{12} = \frac{2}{3}$ and $\frac{XZ}{LN} = \frac{7}{10.5} = \frac{2}{3}$ Since all three ratios are equal, the sides are in proportion.
- All three pairs of corresponding sides are in the same ratio, so the requirement for SSS~ is met, and $\Delta XYZ \sim \Delta LMN$. Remember, you must test all three pairs – the first two pairs could be in the same ratio and the third pair can be in a different ratio, in which case the triangles would not be similar.

• ΔSVA and ΔNWC appear to be similar by AA~. If they are, then two pairs of corresponding angles will have to be congruent.

• $m\angle S + m\angle A + m\angle V = 180°$
$73° + 40° + m\angle V = 180°$, so $m\angle V = 67°$
$m\angle N + m\angle C + m\angle W = 180°$
$73° + m\angle C + 67° = 180°$, so $m\angle C = 40°$

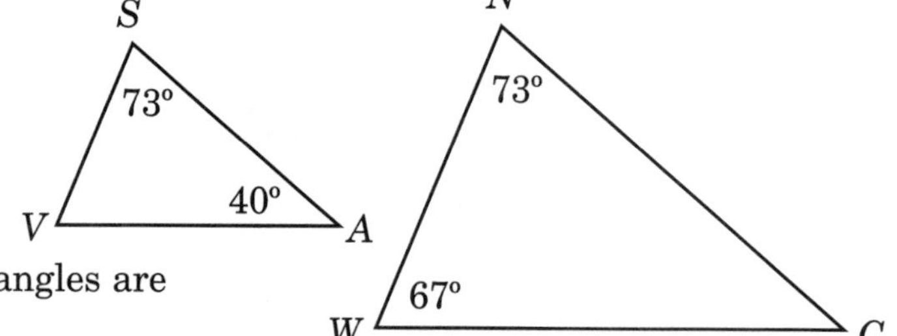

• Since all three pairs of corresponding angles are, therefore, congruent, these triangles are similar by AA~.

• In fact, as soon as it was shown that $m\angle S = m\angle N = 73°$ and $m\angle V = m\angle W = 67°$, AA~ had been satisfied, because only two pairs of corresponding angles must be shown to be congruent the third pair will automatically be congruent if the first two pairs are congruent.

Practice

Determine whether or not each of these pairs of triangles is similar. If they are, state the postulate or theorem that makes them similar.

1.

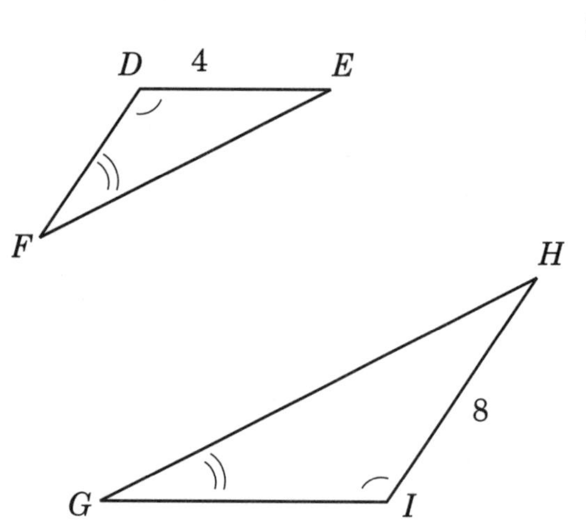

2.

R 20 T 11.2 V

L 25 N 14 P

3.

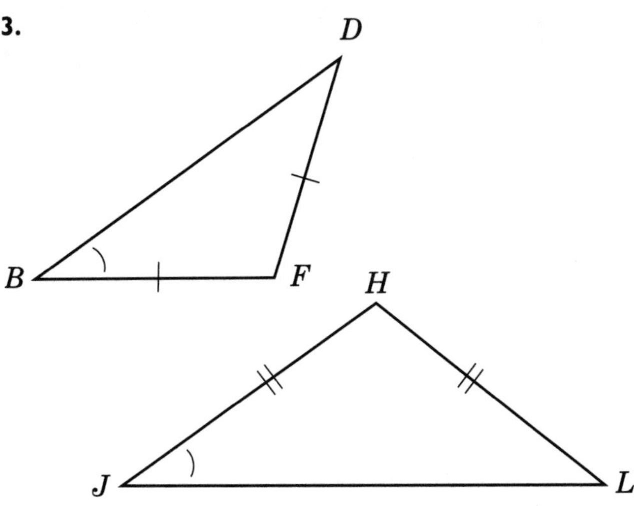
D
B
F
H
J
L

4.

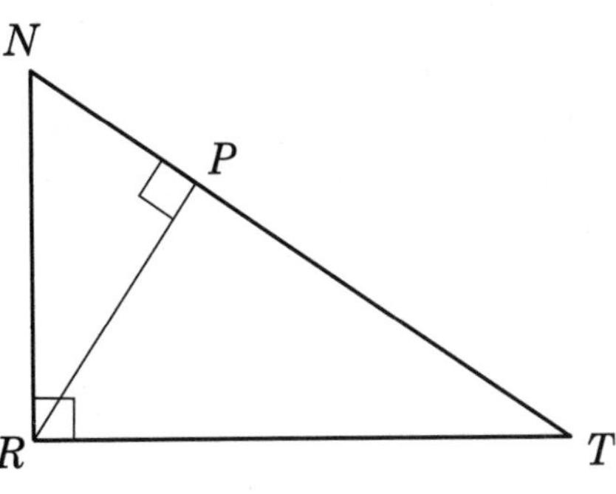
N
P
R
T

5.

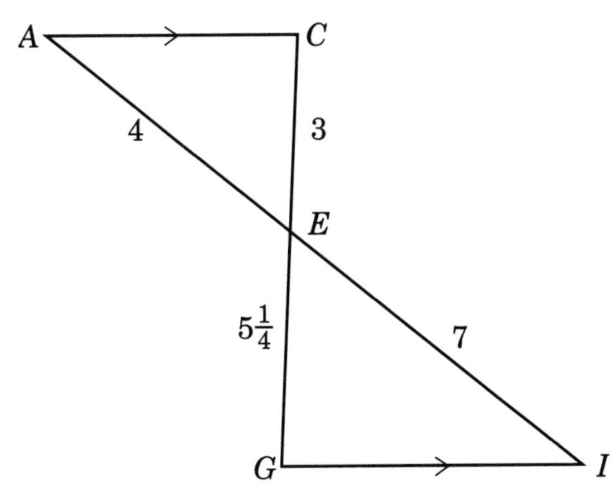
A
C
4
3
E
$5\frac{1}{4}$
7
G
I

6.

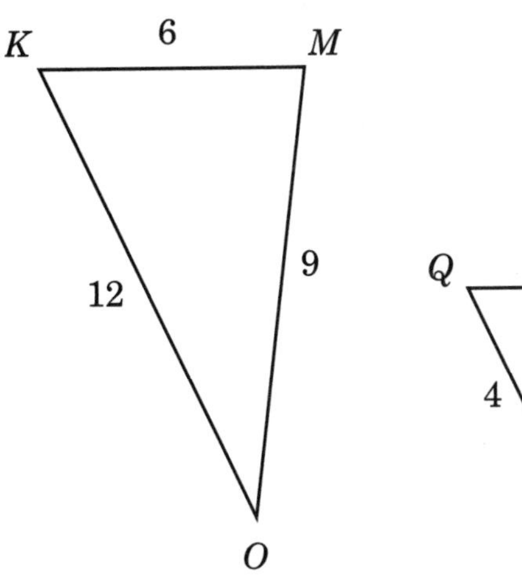
K
6
M
12
9
O

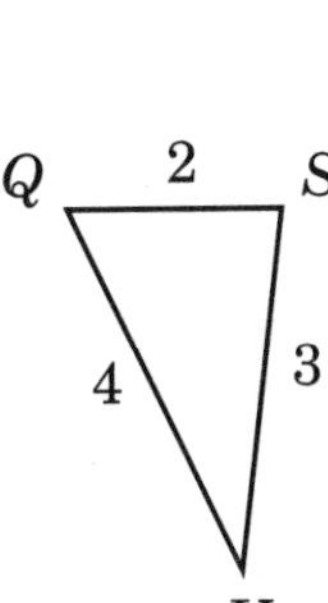
Q
2
S
4
3
U

7.

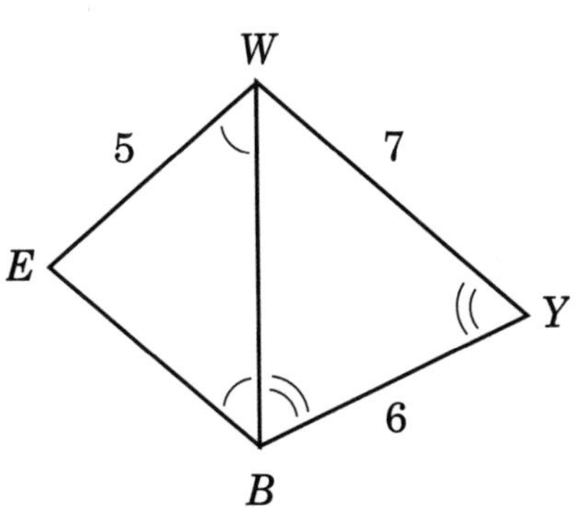
W
5
7
E
Y
6
B

8.

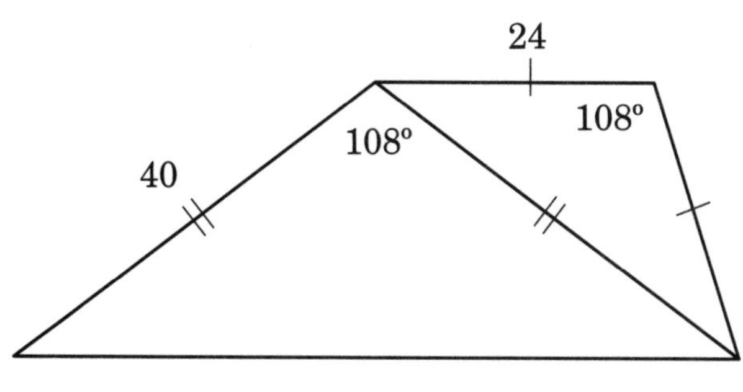
24
108°
108°
40

Finding Measurements in Similar Triangles

If two triangles are similar, you can use the measurements of one to calculate the measurements of the other. You can also use proportions to find the measurements of parts of the triangles.

If we know that $\Delta ABE \sim \Delta ACD$, then the following proportions are true:

$\frac{AE}{AC} = \frac{AB}{BC} = \frac{WB}{DC}$ $\qquad$ $\frac{AE}{ED} = \frac{AB}{BC}$

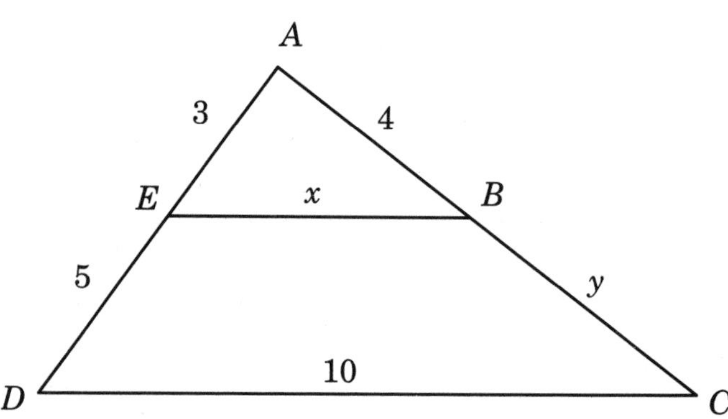

This follows directly from the fact that in similar triangles, the sides are in proportion.
This is based on the Triangle Proportionality Theorem: since $\overline{EB} \| \overline{DC}$, $\overline{EB}$ divides the sides of ΔADC proportionally. This is not helpful if you are trying to find the third sides, however.

These proportions allow us to find the values of x and y.

$$\frac{AE}{AD} = \frac{ED}{DC} \qquad \frac{AE}{ED} = \frac{AE}{ED}$$

$$\frac{3}{8} = \frac{x}{10} \qquad \frac{3}{8} = \frac{4}{y}$$

$$8x = 30 \qquad 3y = 20$$

$$x = 3.75 \qquad y = 6$$

Practice

Find x and y for each of the following pairs of similar triangles.

1.

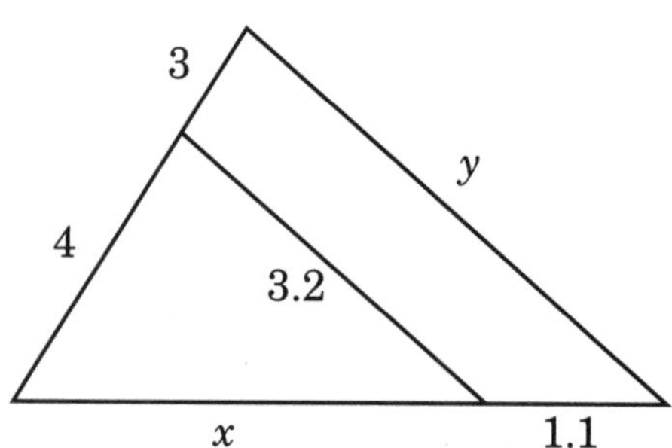

2.

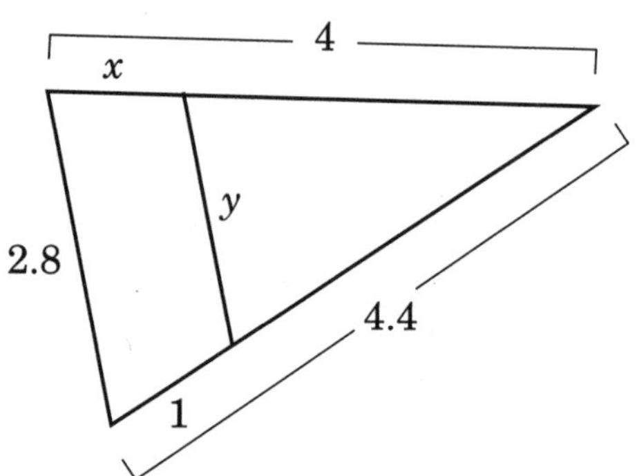

3.

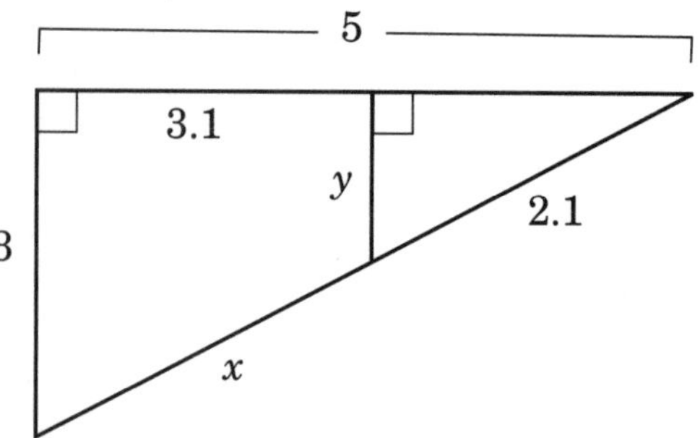

4.

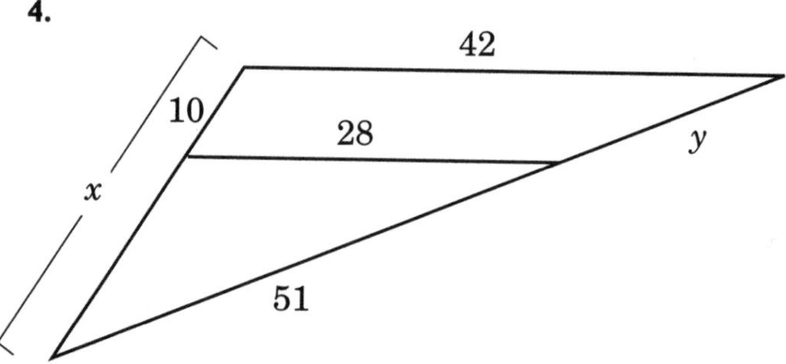

Triangles Exam

Directions:

This exam requires you to put together everything you have learned in this book. Look at each question and think about how you can break it down into steps based on specific topics from the book.

1. Name the vertices and sides of this triangle.
   Find the measures of the acute angles in this picture.
   What kind of triangle is this?
   What type of angle is $\angle CDB$?

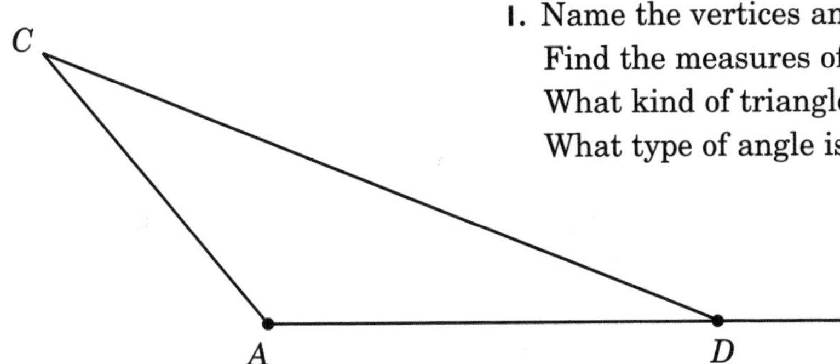

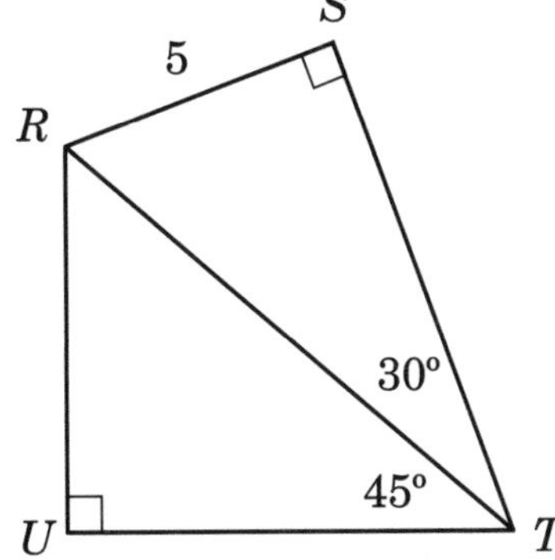

2. Find the length of all segments which aren't shown.
   Find the area of *RSTU*.

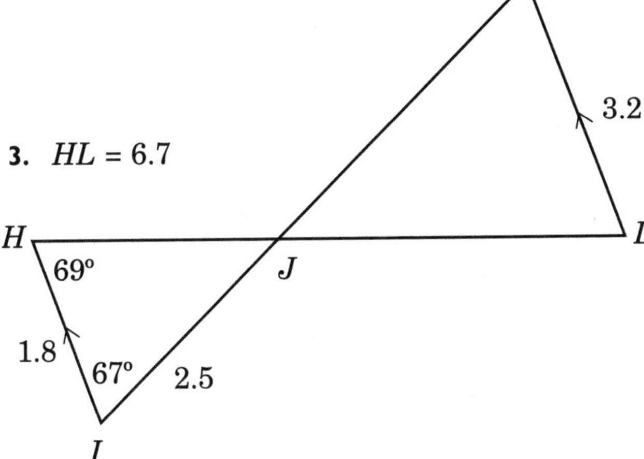

3. $HL = 6.7$

$m\angle HJI =$ $m\angle KJL =$
$m\angle HJK =$ $m\angle JKL =$
$m\angle KLJ =$ $m\angle LJI =$
$HJ =$ $JL =$
$JK =$
Is $\Delta HJI \sim \Delta KLJ$? Why or why not?
Is $\Delta HJI \sim \Delta LJK$? Why or why not?

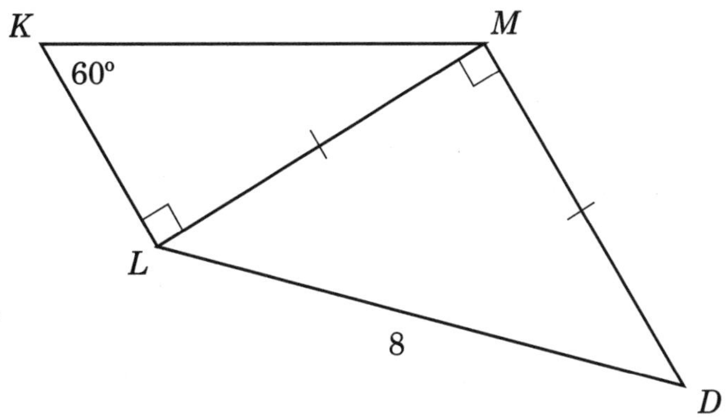

4. $m\angle KML =$
   $m\angle MDL =$
   $m\angle MLD =$ $KL =$
   $LM =$ $LD =$
   $MD =$ $KM =$
   Find the area of *KMDL*.
   Are these triangles similar? Why or why not?
   What is the perimeter of ΔKML? of ΔMLD?
   What is the perimeter of this quadrilateral?

5. $\overline{FB} \cong \overline{FA}$. D is the midpoint of $\overline{AC}$ and E is the midpoint of $\overline{BC}$. Explain why ΔAGB and ΔBGC are similar triangles.
   $\overline{JD}$ is a __________.
   $\overline{BG}$ is a __________.
   $\overline{FE}$ is a __________.
   $\overline{FC}$ is a __________.
   If $AC = 36$, $FE =$ _____.

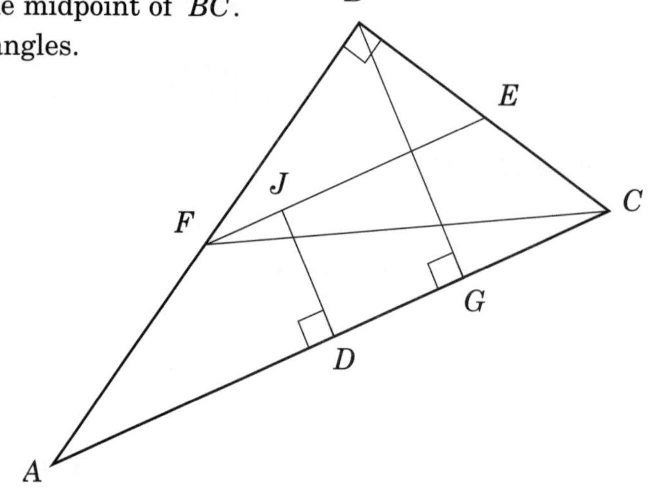

6. How do you know that $\overline{FG}$ is parallel to $\overline{AE}$?
   If $AE = 5$ and $BE = 2$, find the lengths of $\overline{FG}$, $\overline{HG}$ and $\overline{FH}$.
   If the area of ΔBDE is $12u^2$, what is the length of $\overline{DE}$?
   What is the area of parallelogram $ACDB$?

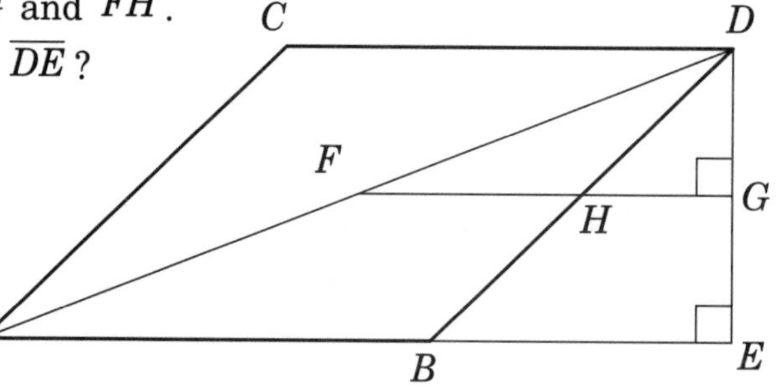

7. One of the base angles of an isosceles triangle has a measure of 60°. If one of the legs of the isosceles triangle is 9 centimeters, find the area of the triangle.

8. $\Delta HQI \cong \Delta MIQ$. Find the missing measurements. What postulate or theorem justifies this congruency, based on the initial information given?

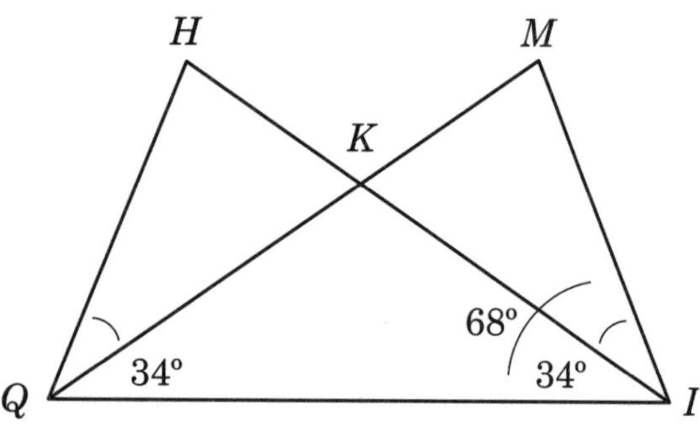

9. $\Delta NXW \sim \Delta ZAT$. Find the missing angle measures, calculate the scale factor and find the missing lengths of sides.

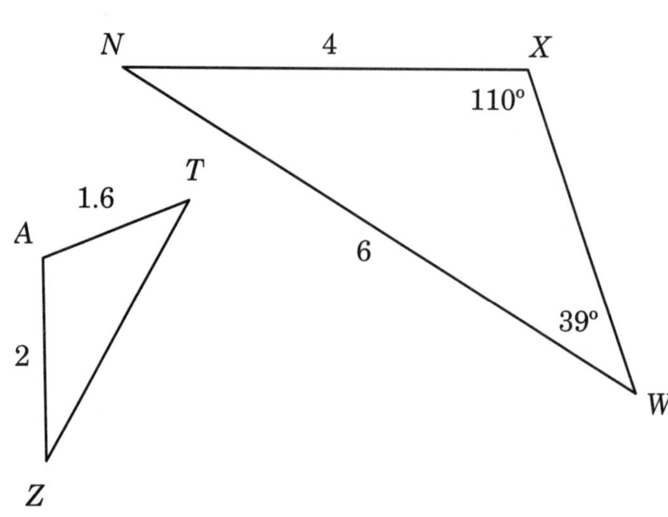

Glossary

Auxiliary Line: A line that is added to a picture. It is sometimes helpful to extend a line or add the ray of an angle to solve a geometric problem. Auxiliary lines are usually dashed so that it is clear that they are not part of the original problem.

Complementary Angles: Two angles whose sum is 90°.

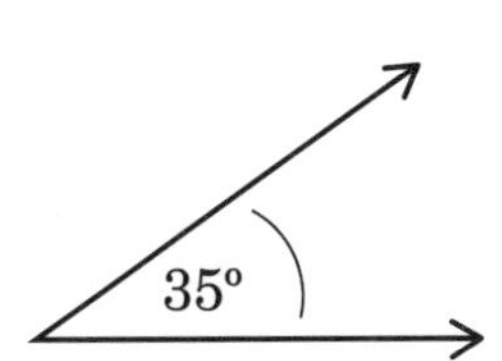

and

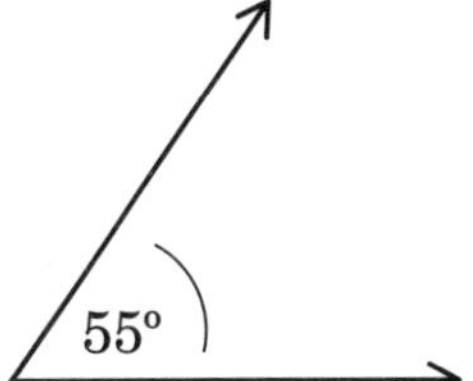

Parallel Lines: Two lines which do not intersect.

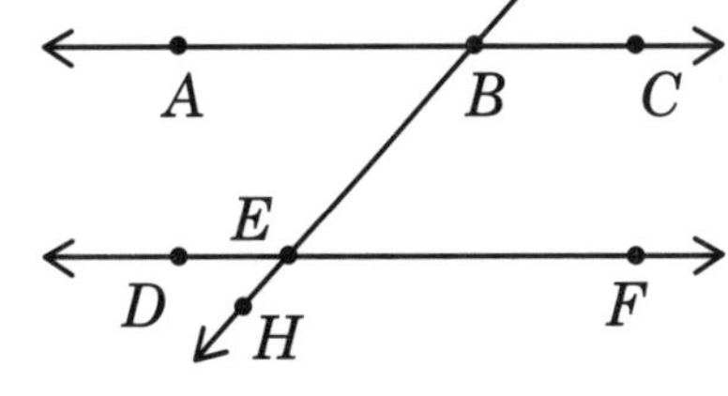

- $\overline{AC} \| \overline{DF}$ is read as "line AC is parallel to line DF."
- $\overline{GH}$ is a transversal because it intersects 2 lines.
- The arrows on the lines show that they are parallel.
- When 2 parallel lines are cut by a transversal:

  a. Alternate interior angles are congruent
  $\angle CBE \cong \angle BED$ and $\angle ABE \cong \angle BEF$.

  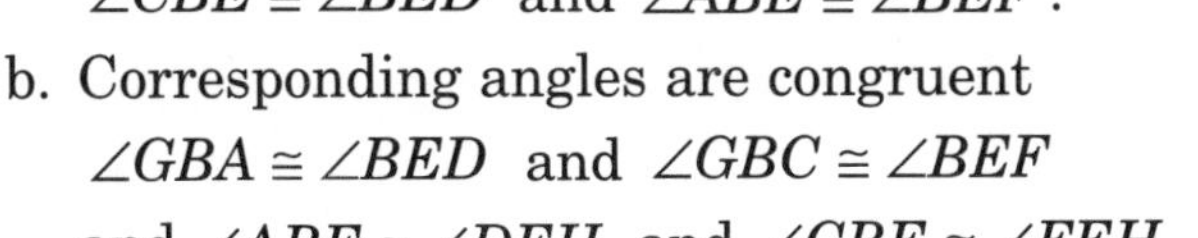

  b. Corresponding angles are congruent
  $\angle GBA \cong \angle BED$ and $\angle GBC \cong \angle BEF$
  and $\angle ABE \cong \angle DEH$ and $\angle CBE \cong \angle FEH$.

  c. Same-side interior angles are supplementary
  $m\angle ABE + m\angle DEB = 180°$ and $m\angle CBE + m\angle FEB = 180°$.

Parallelogram: A quadrilateral in which both pairs of opposite sides are parallel.

- Pairs of opposite sides are congruent.
- Pairs of opposite angles are congruent.
- Diagonals bisect each other.

Rectangle: A parallelogram with 4 right angles.

- All the properties of parallelograms also apply to rectangles.
- Diagonals are congruent to each other.

Square: A rectangle with 4 congruent sides.

- All properties of parallelograms and rectangles apply to squares.
- Diagonals intersect to form right angles.
- Diagonals bisect the angles of the parallelogram.

Symbols: = **equals** ≅ **congruent** ~ **similar** ≈ **approximately**

Supplementary Angles:

- Two angles whose sum is 180º.
- If two adjacent angles form a straight line, they are supplementary. They are called a linear pair.

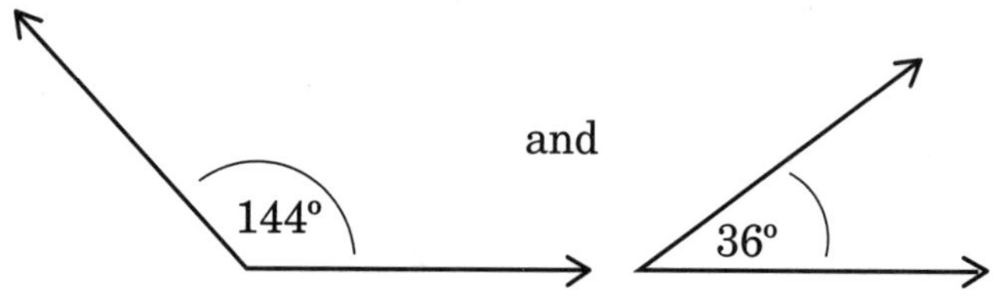

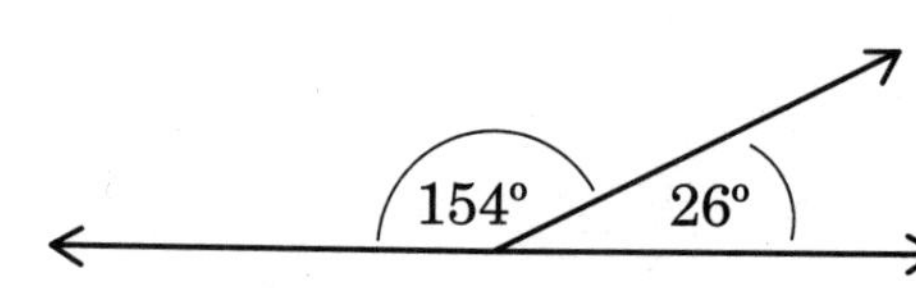

Answer Key

Page 3

There are a variety of correct answers for each problem in this section. Only a few examples will be given for most problems in this key.

1. ΔXYZ or ΔZYX, ΔZXY, ΔYXZ, ΔYZX, ΔXZY
   $\angle X$ or $\angle YXZ$ or $\angle ZXY$
   $\angle Y$ or $\angle ZYX$ or $\angle XYZ$
   $\angle Z$ or $\angle YZX$ or $\angle XZY$
2. ΔLRW, etc.
   $\angle L, \angle R$, $\angle W$, etc.
3. ΔGNK, etc.
   $\angle G$, $\angle N$, $\angle K$, etc.
4. ΔDQA, etc.
   $\angle D$, $\angle Q$, $\angle A$, *etc.*

Page 5

Scalene Obtuse

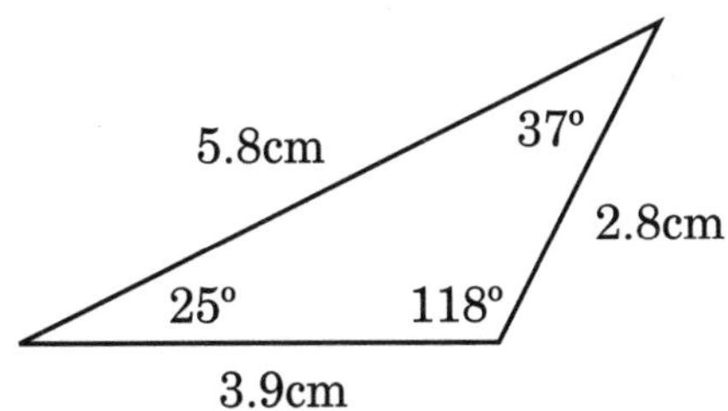

Equilateral Equiangular

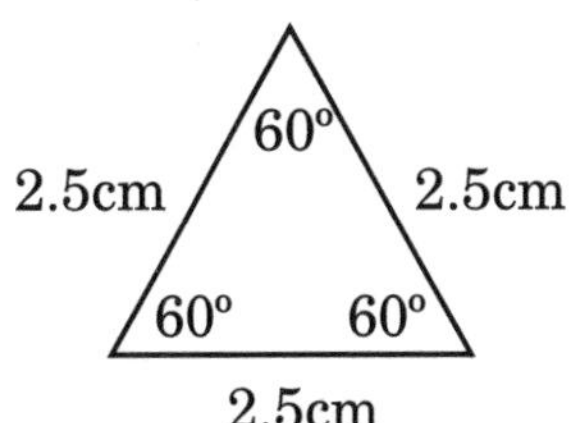

Isosceles Right

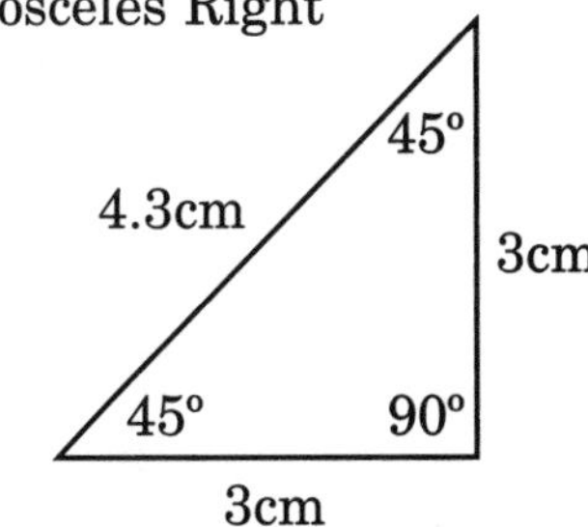

Scalene Acute

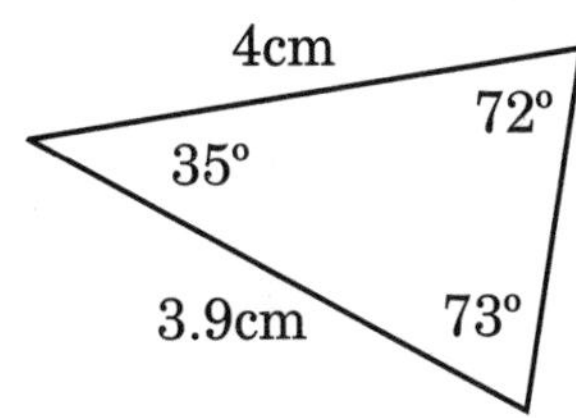

Scalene Obtuse

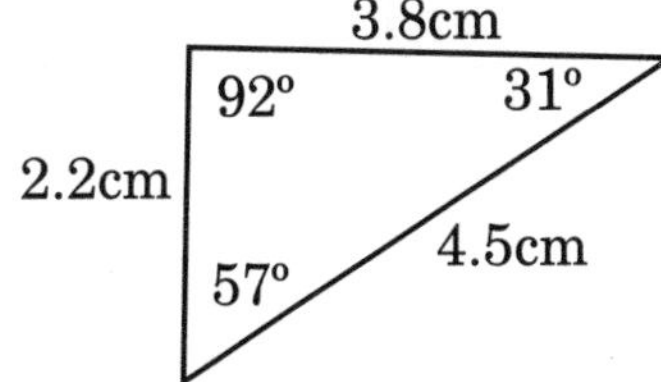

Scalene Obtuse

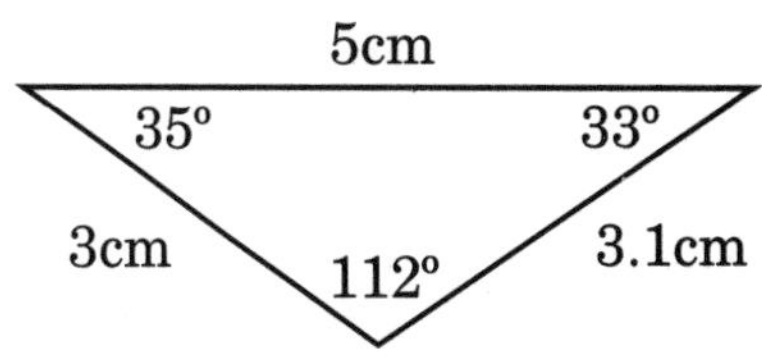

Page 7

1. Scalene—appears also to be obtuse
2. Isosceles—appears also to be acute
3. Equiangular—and therefore, equilateral
4. Isosceles Right
5. Right Triangle
6. Isosceles Triangle

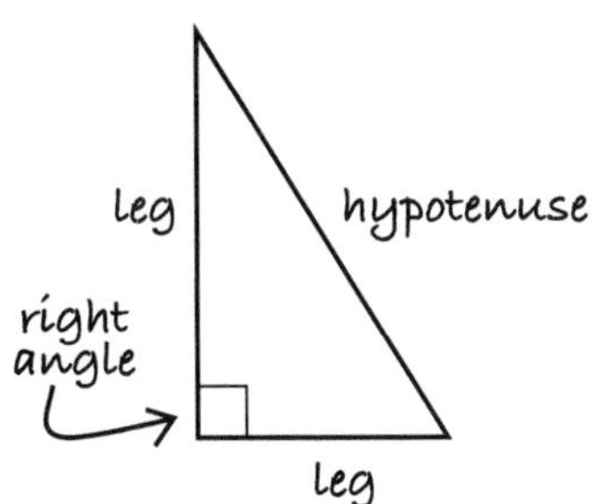

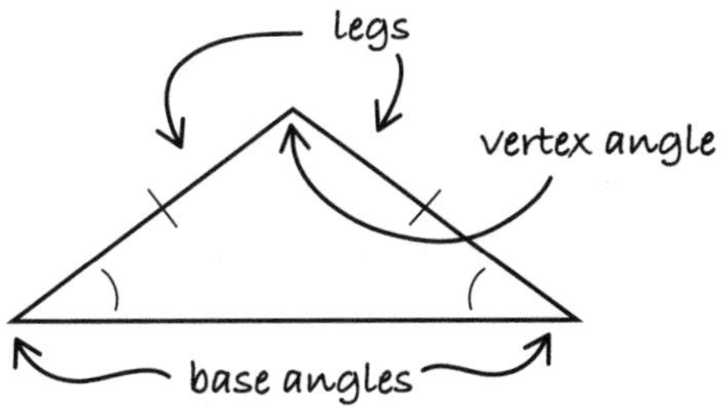

7. Obtuse Scalene

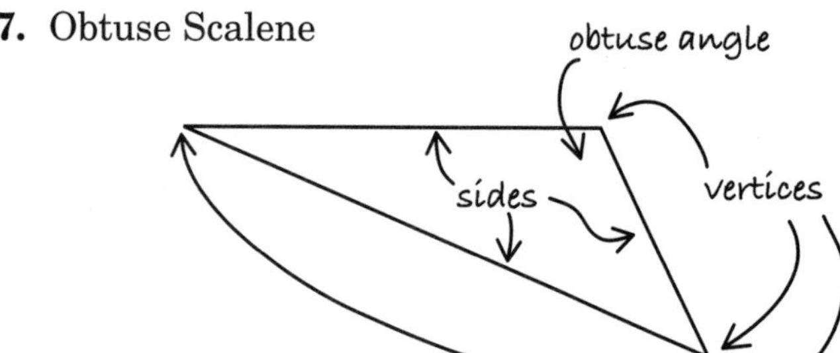

Page 8

1. *Option #1:* Since the angles of a triangle add up to 180°, let x = the angle to be found and then use the equation $108° + 53° + x = 180°$ and solve through $161° + x = 180°$ to find that $x = 19°$.
Option #2: Add up the two angles you know: $108° + 53° = 161°$.
Then realize that if you subtract the sum from 180 you'll find how many degrees are left for the third angle: $180° - 161° = 19°$.

2. *Option #1:* $x + 90 + 35 = 180$
$x + 125 = 180$
$x = 55°$

Option #2: Since the acute angles of a right triangle are complementary
$x + 35 = 90$
$x = 55°$

3. $\angle G$ and $\angle I$ are the base angles of an isosceles triangle and are, therefore, congruent.
So $x + x + 30 = 180$
$2x = 150$
$x = 75°$

4. Just add the angles and set them equal to 180°:
$$2x - 6 + 3x + 1 + 100 = 180$$
$$5x + 95 = 180$$
$$5x = 85$$
$$x = 17°$$
Since $x = 17$, you can substitute back into the expressions to find the measure of each angle:
$m\angle J = 2x - 6 = 2(17) - 6 = 28°$ and $m\angle K = 3x + 1 = 3(17) + 1 = 52°$

5. In an isosceles right triangle, the acute angles are always 45° each (they have to be both congruent and complementary). To see how this works: If you let y be each angle times y since they are congruent, then $y + y = 90°$, so $2y = 90°$, and $y = 45°$.

6. $3x - 4 + 2x + 7 + 4x - 12 = 180$
$9x - 9 = 180$
$9x = 189$
$x = 21$

So... $m\angle Q = 3x - 4 = 3(21) - 4 = 59°$
$m\angle R = 2x + 7 = 2(21) + 7 = 49°$
$m\angle S = 4x - 12 = 4(21) - 12 = 72°$

Page 10

1. Since this is an equiangular triangle, all interior angles measure 60°.
Therefore, $60 + x = 180$ and $x = 120°$.

2. $80 + 60 + y = 180$
$140 + y = 180$
$y = 40°$
$70 + 75 + x = 180$
$145 + x = 180$
$x = 35°$

The unknown angle in the left triangle can be found by subtracting 25 and 80 from 180: 180 – 105 = 75°.

3. $60 + 75 + x = 180$
$135 + x = 180$
$x = 45°$

In the left triangle 180 – (60 + 75) = 180 – 135 = 45°. The top angle of the large triangle then shows that 75 – 45 = 30, so the triangle on the right is $30 + x + y = 180$, or $30 + 45 + y = 180$. Simplifying, $75 + y = 180$, and $y = 105°$. Or, more simply, y and the 75° angle form a straight angle, 180 – 75 = 105°.

4. $180 - 70 = y$ because they form a straight angle, and $y = 110°$. The angle whose measure is $y = 110°$ is an exterior angle with the angles whose measures are $x°$ and 55° as remote interior angles. Therefore $110 = x + 55$ and $x = 55°$.

5. $180 - 57 = y$, so $y = 123°$. The unmarked acute angle is 57° in the triangle, so $90 - 57 = x$ and $x = 33°$, based on the fact that the acute angles of a right triangle are complementary. Or you could approach the problem based on the sum of the remote interior angles equaling the measure of the exterior angle.

6. In the large triangle, there are two angles with measures of $x°$ because this is an isosceles triangle. Therefore, $180 = 65 + 41 + x + x$.

$180 = 106 + 2x$
$74 = 2x$
$x = 37°$

Since the angle whose measure is $y°$ is an exterior angle to 65° and $x°$, $65 + 37 = y$, so $y = 102°$.

7. The angle in the lower right part of the triangle is 100° because it forms a straight angle with the 80° angle. So,

$42 + 100 + y = 180$
$142 + y = 180$
$y = 38°$.

Since alternate interior angles are congruent when parallel lines are cut by a transversal, $x = 42°$.

8. Since alternate interior angles are congruent when parallel lines are cut by a transversal, the angle adjacent to the angle with a measure of $y°$ has a measure of 40°. Therefore $y = 180 - 40 = 140°$. Since the $x°$ and 65° angles are remote interior angles to the exterior angle with measure $y° = 140°$, $140 = 65 + x$, then $x = 75°$. Also, since consecutive angles of a parallelogram are supplementary, $x + 65 + 40 = 180$, also leading to the fact that $x = 75°$.

Page 12

1. $x^2 + x^2 = \left(5\sqrt{2}\right)^2$
$2x^2 = 25 \cdot 2$
$x^2 = 25$
$x = 5$

2. $x^2 + 8^2 = 10^2$
$x^2 + 64 = 100$
$x^2 = 36$
$x = 6$

3. $x^2 + 2^2 = 7^2$
$x^2 + 4 = 49$
$x^2 = 45$
$x = \sqrt{9 \cdot 5}$
$x = 3\sqrt{5}$

4. $4^2 + 3^2 = x^2$
$16 + 9 = x^2$
$25 = x^2$
$x = 5$

5. $24^2 + 7^2 = x^2$
$576 + 49 = x^2$
$625 = x^2$
$x = 25$

6. $8^2 = x^2 + x^2$
$64 = 2x^2$
$32 = x^2$
$x = \sqrt{32}$
$x = \sqrt{16 \cdot 2}$
$x = 4\sqrt{2}$

Page 15

1. The short leg has a length of 4 in this 30–60–90 triangle. Since the length of the long leg is the length of the short leg times $\sqrt{3}$, $x = 4\sqrt{3}$, and the length of the hypotenuse is twice the length of the short leg, $y = 2 \cdot 4 = 8$.
2. This is a 45–45–90 triangle. The length of the hypotenuse equals the length of the leg times $\sqrt{2}$. Since the leg has a length of 3, the hypotenuse is $x = 3\sqrt{2}$.
3. ΔUST is an isosceles right triangle, a 45-45-90 triangle. The hypotenuse has a length of 10. So $x\sqrt{2} = 10$ and $x = \frac{10}{\sqrt{2}} \cdot \frac{\sqrt{2}}{\sqrt{2}} = \frac{10\sqrt{2}}{2} = 5\sqrt{2}$.
4. ΔABD and ΔCBD are congruent 30–60–90 triangles. The short leg has a length of x which must be half of the hypotenuse: $2x = 12$, and $x = 6$. The long leg has a length of $y = 6\sqrt{3}$.
5. This is an equilateral triangle since $m\angle LMN = 60$, and $\angle MLN \cong \angle MNL$ because it is an isosceles triangle. Therefore there are two 30–60–90 triangles inside the larger triangle. $LN = 12 = MN$ and is the hypotenuse. $12 = 2PN$, so $PN = 6$. The longer leg length is $x = 6\sqrt{3}$.
6. ΔDEF is an isosceles right triangle, so $m\angle EDF = m\angle EFD = 45°$.

$$m\angle EFD + m\angle DFG = m\angle GFE$$
$$45 + m\angle DFG = 105$$
$$m\angle DFG = 60°$$
$$m\angle GDF = 30° \text{ and } x = 30 + 45 = 75°.$$

Therefore $\overline{GF}$ is the short leg. $\overline{DG}$ is the long leg, and $GF \cdot \sqrt{3} = 7\sqrt{3}$ and $GF = 7$. $\overline{DF}$ is the hypotenuse, so $DF = 2 \cdot 7 = 14$. $\overline{DF}$ is also the hypotenuse of ΔDFE, so $y = \frac{14}{\sqrt{2}} \cdot \frac{\sqrt{2}}{\sqrt{2}} = \frac{14\sqrt{2}}{2} = 7\sqrt{2}$.

Page 18

1. $3 + 10 + 9 = 22$.
2. $AC = CB = 5$, so $5 + 5 + 8 = 18$.
3. $35a + 25a + 10 = 60a + 10$ (remember, you can only add like terms).
4. Since it's a parallelogram, opposite sides are congruent, and $JI = 15$. $15 + 6 + 17 = 38$.
5. 7" + 9" + 8" = 24".
6. 1m = 100cm, so 100cm + 75cm + 45cm = 220cm or 2.2 m.
7. ΔADC has a perimeter of $4 + 1.5 + 3.1 = 8.6$; ΔADB has a perimeter of $4 + 1.5 + 3.5 + 3.8 = 12.8$; and ΔACB has a perimeter of $3.1 + 3.8 + 3.5 = 10.4$.
8. $YZ + ZX + YX = 27$, but $YZ = ZX$, so they can be substituted for each other. $YZ + YZ + 11 = 27$, so $2YZ = 16$ and $YZ = 8$.

Page 20

1. $b = 8$, $h = 3$ so $A = \frac{1}{2}bh = \frac{1}{2} \cdot 8 \cdot 3 = 12$.
2. $b = 3$, $h = 4$ so $A = \frac{1}{2}bh = \frac{1}{2} \cdot 3 \cdot 4 = 6$.

3. Since this is a rectangle, the angles are right angles. First find the length of $\overline{AD}$.

$$13^2 = 5^2 + AD^2$$
$$169 = 25 + AD^2$$
$$144 = AD^2$$
$$12 = AD$$

$$b = 12,\ h = 5$$
$$A = \tfrac{1}{2}bh$$
$$A = \tfrac{1}{2} \cdot 5 \cdot 12$$
$$A = 30$$

4. If x is the length of an altitude, then:

$$10^2 = 3^2 = x^2$$
$$100 = 9 + x$$
$$91 = x^2$$
$$\sqrt{91} = x$$

$$b = 14,\ \text{h} = \sqrt{91}$$
$$A = \tfrac{1}{2}bh$$
$$A = \tfrac{1}{2} \cdot 14 \cdot \sqrt{91}$$
$$A = 7\sqrt{91} \approx 66.8$$

5. $b = 33$, $h = 22$, so:

$$A = \tfrac{1}{2}bh$$
$$A = \tfrac{1}{2} \cdot 33 \cdot 22$$
$$A = 363$$

6. The diagonals of a rhombus intersect to form right angles. So there are 4 right angles in the rhombus.

$$8^2 = 7^2 + AE^2$$
$$64 = 49 + AE^2$$
$$15 = AE^2$$
$$\sqrt{15} = AE$$

$AC = 2\sqrt{15}$, because AC is twice AE. $b = 2\sqrt{15}$, $h = 7$.

$$A = \tfrac{1}{2}bh$$
$$A = \tfrac{1}{2} \cdot 2\sqrt{15} \cdot 7$$
$$A = 7\sqrt{15} \approx 27.1$$

7.

$$10^2 = 8^2 + BD^2$$
$$100 = 64 + BD^2$$
$$36 = BD^2,$$

$BD = 6$ and $BC = 12$

$$b = 12,\ h = 8$$
$$A = \tfrac{1}{2}bh$$
$$A = \tfrac{1}{2} \cdot 12 \cdot 8$$
$$A = 48$$

8. To find the area of any of these triangles, it is first necessary to find the missing lengths.

$$7^2 + BD^2 = 15^2$$
$$49 + BD^2 = 225$$
$$BD^2 = 176$$
$$BD = 4\sqrt{11}$$

$$AB^2 + 7^2 = \sqrt{445}^2$$
$$AB^2 + 49 = 445$$
$$AB^2 = 396$$
$$AB = 6\sqrt{11}$$

$$A\triangle CBD = \tfrac{1}{2} \cdot 4\sqrt{11} \cdot 7 = 14\sqrt{11}$$
$$A\triangle ABC = \tfrac{1}{2} \cdot 6\sqrt{11} \cdot 7 = 21\sqrt{11}$$
$$A\triangle ADC = \tfrac{1}{2} \cdot \left(6\sqrt{11} + 4\sqrt{11}\right) \cdot 7$$
$$= \tfrac{1}{2} \cdot \left(10\sqrt{11}\right) \cdot 7 = 35\sqrt{11} \approx 116.1$$

Page 23

1.

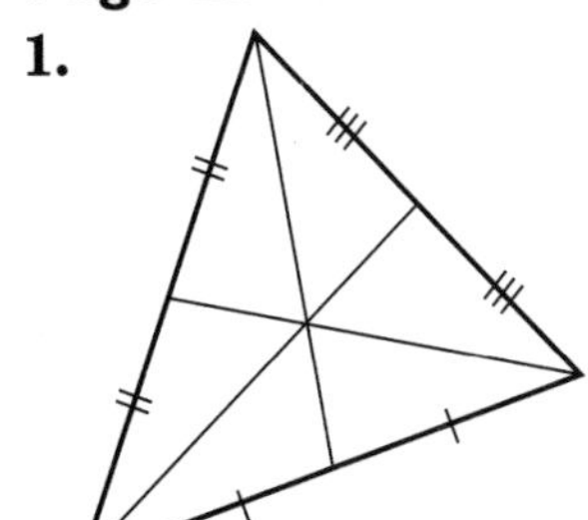

2.

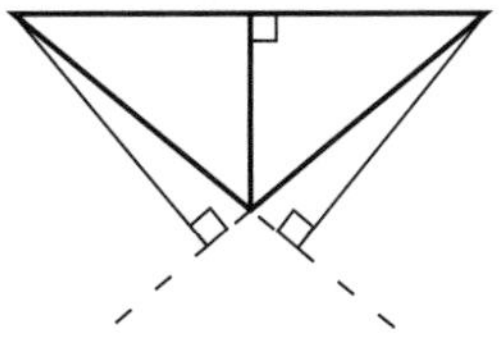

3.

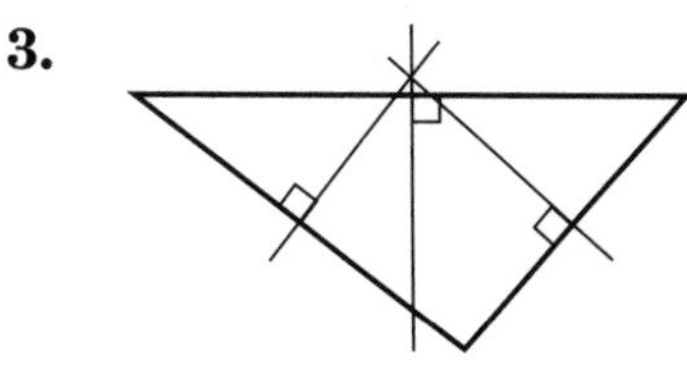

4.

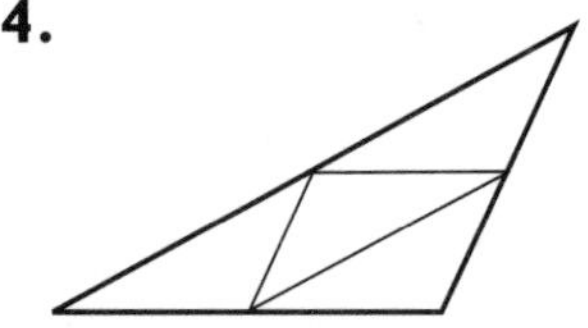

5.

Pages 27–28

1. Since $\angle A \cong \angle B$, this is an isosceles triangle with $CB = 7$. Since $\overline{CD}$ is the altitude from the vertex of an isosceles triangle, it is also a median. So, $AD = \frac{1}{2}(12) = 6$ and $DB = AD = 6$.
2. YQ is the geometric mean of XQ and QZ, so $YQ = \sqrt{6 \cdot 10} = 2\sqrt{15}$.
   ZY is the geometric mean of ZQ and ZX, so $ZY = \sqrt{10 \cdot 16} = 4\sqrt{10}$.
   XY is the geometric mean of XQ and XZ, so $XY = \sqrt{6 \cdot 16} = 4\sqrt{6}$.
3. J is the midpoint of $\overline{KM}$, $\overline{LJ}$ is the median from the right angle of a right triangle and it is congruent to $\overline{KJ}$ and $\overline{JM}$.

   $KM^2 = LM^2 + LK^2$
   $KM^2 = 12^2 + 5^2 = 144 + 25$
   $KM^2 = 169$
   $KM = 13$

   $KJ = JM$
   $JM = 6\frac{1}{2}$
   $JL = 6\frac{1}{2}$

   $KJ = \frac{1}{2}KM$
   $KJ = \frac{1}{2}(13)$
   $KJ = 6\frac{1}{2}$
4. $GH = \frac{1}{2}FE = \frac{1}{2}(17) = 8\frac{1}{2}$. $\overline{GH} \parallel \overline{FE}$ because $\overline{GH}$ is a midsegment.
5. $KL = 4$ because $KL = \frac{1}{2}NM$ (because K and L are midpoints and $\overline{KL}$ is the third side of ΔJKL).
   $JK = 3$ because K is a midpoint, so the height of $\Delta JKL = 3$. $A = \frac{1}{2}bh$
   $A = \frac{1}{2}(4)(3)$
   $A = 6$
6. Since $\overline{SU}$ is a median from the vertex of an isosceles triangle, it is also an altitude. Thus, $m\angle SUT = 90°$. Since ΔRST is an isosceles right triangle, the base angles are each 45°, so $m\angle T = 45°$. If $RT = 20$, then $RU = UT = 10$. Since the median from the right angle of a right triangle is congruent to the halves of the hypotenuse, $SU = 10$ also.
7. **a.** $PL = LO = 3$, so $PO = 6$

   $PO^2 + PQ^2 = OQ^2$
   $6^2 + 8^2 = OQ^2$
   $36 + 64 = OQ^2$
   $100 = OQ^2$
   $OQ = 10$

   $OM = \frac{1}{2}OQ$
   $OM = \frac{1}{2}(10)$
   $OM = 5$

   $LK = PQ = 8$

   $MK = \frac{1}{2}(8)$
   $MK = 4$

   b. $\Delta OQN, b = ON = 8$
   $h = QN = 6$

   $A = \frac{1}{2}bh$
   $A = \frac{1}{2}(8)(6)$
   $A = 24$

   c. *Option #1* The area of a rectangle is base times height, and $b = 8$, $h = 6$
   $A_{NOPQ} = (8)(6) = 48$.

   Option #2 Rectangle $PQNO$ contains ΔPQO and ΔNOQ which are congruent to each other. Since $A_{\Delta OQN} = 24$, $A_{\Delta PQO} = 24$ and
   $A_{NOPQ} = A_{\Delta OQN} + A_{\Delta PQO} = 24 + 24 = 48$.

d. ΔMQK $b = 4, h = 3$

$$A = \tfrac{1}{2}bh$$
$$A = \tfrac{1}{2}(4)(3)$$
$$A = 6$$

e. Quadrilateral *OMKN* can be formed by removing ΔMQK from ΔOQN. We have determined that the area of ΔOQN is 24 and that the area of ΔMQK is 6. Therefore, 24 – 6 = 18: the areas remaining (18) for quadrilateral *OMKN* after subtracting the areas of ΔMQK (6) from the area of ΔOQM (24).

8. a. ΔSRQ has an area of 84. $b = SR = ST + TR = 15 + 6 = 21$. $h = QR$

$$\text{A} = \tfrac{1}{2}\text{bh}$$
$$84 = \tfrac{1}{2}(21)(h)$$
$$168 = 21h$$
$$h = 8$$
$$RQ = 8$$

b. $A_{\Delta SQR} - A_{\Delta QTR} = A_{\Delta STQ}$ $\quad A_{\Delta \text{QTR}} = \tfrac{1}{2}(6)(8) = 24$

$$84 - 24 = 60$$

c. If $PS = 10$ and $PU = 5$, then U is a midpoint of $\overline{PS}$. Since V is also a midpoint, $\overline{UV}$ is a midpoint connector and is, therefore, half the length of $\overline{PQ}$. $PQ = 15$ because *PQTS* is a parallelogram and opposite sides are congruent. $UV = \tfrac{1}{2}(15) = 7\tfrac{1}{2}$

Page 30

1. If the longest leg is $4\sqrt{3}$ then the shortest leg is 4. Since they form a right angle, they can be used to find the area. $A = \tfrac{1}{2}\left(4\sqrt{3}\right)(4) = 8\sqrt{3}$.

2. The altitude to the base of the isosceles triangle will also be a median, and its length can be found: $5^2 = \left(\tfrac{9}{2}\right)^2 + x^2$ (if x is the length of the altitude).

$$25 = \tfrac{81}{4} + x^2$$
$$\frac{100}{4} - \frac{81}{4} = \frac{19}{4}$$

So, $\tfrac{19}{4} = x^2$, and $x = \frac{\sqrt{19}}{2}$ which is the height of the triangle.

The base of the triangle is 9. $A = \tfrac{1}{2} \cdot 9 \cdot \frac{\sqrt{19}}{2} = \frac{9\sqrt{19}}{4}$.

3. The diagonal of a square divides it into two 45–45–90 triangles. The diagonal is the hypotenuse of each triangle, so the legs can be found: $A = \frac{24}{\sqrt{2}} \cdot \frac{\sqrt{2}}{\sqrt{2}} = \frac{24\sqrt{2}}{2} = 12\sqrt{2}$.

Option #1: Since the legs are perpendicular, they can be used as the base and height of each triangle. $A_\Delta = \tfrac{1}{2}\left(12\sqrt{2}\right)\left(12\sqrt{2}\right) = \left(6\sqrt{2}\right)\left(12\sqrt{2}\right) = 72 \cdot 2 = 144$. Since there are two congruent triangles, the area of the square is $144 \cdot 2 = 288$.

Option #2: Since the area of a rectangle is just base times height, and the legs can be the base and height, the area of the square is $\left(12\sqrt{2}\right)\left(12\sqrt{2}\right) = 144 \cdot 2 = 288$.

4. Since the base angles are 30º, the vertex angle has to be 120º. That angle will be bisected by an altitude drawn to the base because that altitude will also be a median and an angle-bisector. That will create two congruent 30–60–90 triangles for which the hypotenuse is 8cm. Therefore the short leg (which is the altitude, and therefore the height, of the original triangle) is 4cm and the long leg (half the base of the original triangle) is $4\sqrt{3}$ cm. The base of the original triangle is $2 \cdot 4\sqrt{3}$cm or $8\sqrt{3}$ cm. The area of the triangle is $\frac{1}{2}(4\text{cm})(8\sqrt{3}\text{cm}) = 16\sqrt{3}\text{cm}^2$.

5. If you draw a line that intersects the edge of every step, a large right rectangle is formed: 8 small and congruent right triangles, and one rectangular region. If you find the area of each region and add them together, you'll be able to calculate how many gallons of paint will be needed.

A. Find the dimensions and area of each of the 8 small triangles.
Each has a leg that is 9" and a leg that is 12". Therefore their hypotenuse is found:

$$9^2 + 12^2 = h^2$$
$$81 + 144 = h^2$$
$$225 = h^2$$
$$h = 15$$

Each small right triangle has an area of $\frac{1}{2}(9)(12) = 54\text{in}^2$; all 8 triangles together have an area of $8 \cdot 54\text{in}^2 = 432\text{in}^2$.

B. Find the dimensions and area of the large right triangle. Since the hypotenuses of the 8 triangles form the hypotenuse of the large triangle, the hypotenuse of the large triangle is 8 · 15" = 120". The vertical leg of the large right triangle is the sum of all of the heights of the small right triangles. Thus, the vertical leg has a length of 8 · 9" = 72". The horizontal leg of the large right triangle is the sum of the horizontal legs of the small right triangles. The horizontal leg is 8 · 12" = 96". The area of the large right triangle is 96" · 72" = 6912 in^2.

C. Find the dimensions and area of the rectangular region.
The rectangular region's horizontal length is the same length as the horizontal leg of the large right triangle: 96". The rectangular region's vertical length is 9 inches less than 8 feet. 8 feet is 8 · 12" = 96 inches. 96" – 9" = 87". The area of the rectangular region is 96" · 87" = 8352in^2.

D. Add the areas of the three regions together. $432\text{in}^2 + 6912\text{in}^2 + 8352\text{in}^2 = 15696\text{in}^2$. But we need to know the area in feet^2 because that's how we know about the paint. A square foot is 12 inches by 12 inches...so it is 144in^2. Iif we divide the 15696in^2 by 144in^2, we'll have our area in ft^2. The area of the wall is 109ft^2. Since 1 gallon of paint will cover 150ft^2, we will only need 1 gallon and we will have some left over.

Page 31

1. Statement: $\Delta FGH \cong \Delta KIJ$ Parts: $\overline{FG} \cong \overline{KI}, \overline{GH} \cong \overline{IJ}, \overline{FH} \cong \overline{KJ}, \angle F \cong \angle K, \angle G \cong \angle I, \angle H \cong \angle J$

2. Statement: $\Delta BDF \cong \Delta JLH$ Parts: $\overline{BD} \cong \overline{JL}, \overline{DF} \cong \overline{LH}, \overline{BF} \cong \overline{JH}, \angle D \cong \angle L, \angle F \cong \angle H, \angle B \cong \angle J$

p. 32

1. Since $\angle K$ corresponds to $\angle Y$, m$\angle K$ = 87°. Since $\angle O$ corresponds to $\angle T$, m$\angle O$ = 41°. Since there are 180° in a triangle, $m\angle E = m\angle C$ = 180 – (41 + 87) = 52°. Since $\overline{ET}$ corresponds to $\overline{CO}$, CO= 29. Since $\overline{KT}$ corresponds to $\overline{OY}$, KT = 28. Since $\overline{EK}$ corresponds to $\overline{CY}$, EK = 20.
2. $WI = QS = 2.5$ $IM = SL = 2.5$ $WM = LQ = 2$
   $m\angle W = m\angle Q = 65°$ $m\angle M = m\angle L = 65°$ $m\angle I = m\angle S = 180 - (65 + 65) = 50°$
3. $CN = BR = 5$ $CZ = ZR = 2.1$ $NZ = ZB = 3.9$
   $m\angle C = m\angle R = 50°$ $m\angle N = m\angle B = 23°$ $m\angle CZN = m\angle RZB = 107°$
4. $DA = XH = 2.5$ $DH = AX = 2$ $m\angle DAH = m\angle XHA = 50°$
   $m\angle X = m\angle D = 50°$ $m\angle XAH = m\angle DHA =80°$
5. $VU = VI = UK = IK = 6$ (corresponding parts and isosceles triangles)
   $m\angle KUI = m\angle VUI = m\angle VIU = m\angle KIU = 74°$ $m\angle V = m\angle K = 32°$
6. $WE = RE = 3$ $EQ = ET = 7.5$ $WQ = TR = 2.5$
   $m\angle WEQ = m\angle RET = 53°$ (corresponding parts and vertical angles)
   $m\angle W = m\angle R = 75°$ $m\angle Q = m\angle T = 52°$

Pages 34–35

1. SSS; $\Delta IJR \cong \Delta MDU$ (and since you know that these are right triangles, you could also prove them congruent using SAS, ASA, HL or AAS).
2. AAS; $\Delta BTK \cong \Delta WNE$ (and since you know that if 2 pairs of angles are congruent, then the third pair is congruent, you could also prove them to be congruent using ASA).
3. Not congruent; $HP \neq CS$.
4. HL; ΔYIQ $\cong \Delta LBV$.
5. SAS; $\Delta ZAR \cong \Delta FAM$ (you can't use ASA because you only know about an additional angle in one of the two triangles).
6. ASA; $\Delta RXH \cong \Delta WTD$ (and since you know that if 2 pairs of angles are congruent, then the third pair is congruent, you could also prove them to be congruent using AAS).
7. AAS; $\Delta BLS \cong \Delta CAJ$ (this cannot be HL because you don't know anything about any of the legs; the presence of a right angle does not guarantee that HL will be appropriate).
8. Not congruent; the sides that are congruent are in the right positions with regard to the angle pair that is known to be congruent.

Page 36

1. $\angle K$ and $\angle R$ are alternate interior angles; since they are congruent, $\overline{HK}$ must be parallel to $\overline{RA}$, which makes $\angle H \cong \angle A$. $\angle HNK \cong \angle ANR$ because vertical angles are congruent. Since N is the midpoint of $\overline{AH}$, $KN = RN$. So these can be proven to be congruent using ASA or AAS. $\Delta HKN \cong \Delta ARN$.
2. Since $FNVL$ is a rectangle, opposite sides are congruent and the angles are right angles. Options for proving them congruent include HL and SSS. Also, the diagonal is a transversal cutting parallel lines, so the alternate interior angles are congruent. Therefore, AAS, SAS, and ASA are also options. $\Delta FNV \cong \Delta VLF$.

3. Since there are 180° in a triangle, $m\angle F = 180 - (75 + 75) = 30$. Also, since $\angle T \cong \angle D$, they each measure 75°. Therefore, since the two triangles have a congruent segment, ASA and AAS both prove these triangles to be congruent. $\Delta TDL \cong \Delta ZPF$.
4. ΔCMU and ΔGUM share $\overline{MU}$. They also have a pair of congruent angles and a pair of congruent sides. But those parts lead only to a SSA, which doesn't exist. However, $\angle CRM \cong \angle URG$ because they are vertical angles, which makes $\Delta CRM \cong \Delta URG$ by AAS. Once you know that those small triangles are congruent you can conclude that $RM = RU$ (so ΔRMU is an isosceles triangle and $\angle RUM \cong \angle RMU$ since they are the base angles) and that $\angle RUG \cong \angle RMC$ because they are corresponding parts of congruent triangles. Therefore $\angle RUG + \angle RUM \cong \angle RMC + \angle RMU$ and $\angle CMU \cong \angle GUM$. Therefore $\Delta CMU \cong \Delta GUM$ by ASA or AAS.
5. Since $\overline{YD} \parallel \overline{VT}$, $\angle DYT \cong \angle VTY$. Since the triangles share $\overline{YT}$, $\Delta DYT \cong \Delta VTY$ by ASA. For a different approach, since $\angle VYT \cong \angle DTY$, $\overline{VY} \parallel \overline{DT}$ and $DYTV$ is a parallelogram because both pairs of opposite sides are parallel. Therefore both pairs of opposite sides are congruent; these triangles can then be proven to be congruent by SAS, SSS, or AAS (if you point out that the opposite angles of a parallelogram are congruent).
6. If two angles of a triangle are congruent to two angles of another triangle, then their third angles are congruent. Therefore $m\angle BTK$ must be 129°. Since these triangles also have a pair of congruent sides, $\Delta BTK \cong \Delta NWK$ by AAS or ASA.
7. If a segment bisects the vertex angle of an isosceles triangle, then it is also a median and an altitude. Therefore $\angle UCJ$ and $\angle UCN$ are right angles and $JC = CN$. And further, $\Delta JCU \cong \Delta NCU$ by HL or SAS (they share a side), or AAS (the base angles are also congruent), or SSS, or ASA.
8. Since $EIOD$ is a square, $ED = IO$ and $\angle EDK$ and $\angle IOV$ are both right angles. Since $EKVI$ is an isosceles trapezoid, $EK = IV$ and $\angle K \cong \angle V$. So $\Delta EKD \cong \Delta IVO$ by HL. Since $\angle KED$ has to be congruent to $\angle VIO$, they can also be proven to be congruent with ASA or AAS.

Page 38

Use the congruency statements to line up corresponding vertices; that gives a reference point for finding missing angles and determining the scale factor.

1. a. $m\angle L = 33°$, $m\angle K = 31°$, $m\angle N = 116°$.
   b. 20:35 = 4:7.
   c. $\frac{4}{7} = \frac{12}{NM}$, so $4NM = 84$ and $NM = 2$; the measures of $\overline{JK}$ and $\overline{NO}$ cannot be determined from the given information.
2. a. $m\angle ACD = 90°$, $m\angle IGC = 49°$, $m\angle ADC = 41°$.
   b. 51:5 = 3:1.
   c. $GC = 3$, $DC = 12$, $DG = 12 - 3 = 9$. (Note: This figure was not drawn to scale.)
3. a. $m\angle RSU = 90°$, $m\angle UST = 150 - 90 = 60$, $m\angle SUT = 90°$, $m\angle T = 30°$.
   b. $\overline{RS}$ is the shortest side of a 30–60–90 triangle; it is half the length of the hypotenuse $RS = 3$. $\overline{US}$ is the shortest side of the large 30–60–90 triangle and it can be used to find the scale factor: $3:3\sqrt{3}$.
   c. $\frac{3}{3\sqrt{3}} = \frac{6}{ST}$ and $ST = 6\sqrt{3}$; $\frac{3}{3\sqrt{3}} = \frac{3\sqrt{3}}{UT}$ and $UT = 9$.

4. a. $m\angle M = 39°$, $m\angle L = 108°$, $m\angle R = 39°$, $m\angle H = 33°$.

   b. 29:40.

   c. $LH = \frac{174}{5} = 34.8$; $GM = \frac{2000}{29} \approx 70$.

Pages 40–41

1. For the purposes of determining similarity, the measures of the sides are irrelevant in this problem. $\Delta FDE \sim \Delta GIH$ by AA~.
2. $\frac{20}{25} = \frac{4}{5} = .8$ and $\frac{11.2}{14} = .8$, so these pairs of sides are in proportion. The angle between them is a right angle in each case, so $\Delta RTV \sim LNP$ by ASA ~.
3. These are both isosceles triangles, having congruent base angles: since $\angle B \cong \angle D$, $\angle B \cong \angle J$, and $\angle L \cong \angle J$, the Transitive Property allows the conclusion that $\angle D \cong \angle L$. Since two pairs of angles of one triangle are congruent to two pairs of angles of another triangle, their third pairs of angles is congruent. So $\Delta BDF \sim \Delta JLH$ are similar by AA~.
4. There are really three similar triangles here: $\Delta NPR \sim \Delta RPT \sim \Delta NRT$. They are all right triangles. In addition to each case, the triangles have an overlapping angle, which makes their third pair of angles congruent. All three are similar by AA~. As an extension, it is true that whenever the altitude is drawn to the hypotenuse of a right triangle, it forms three similar triangles.
5. $\Delta ACE \sim \Delta IGE$ based on AA~ because of alternate interior angles and vertical angles. But SAS also applies because $\frac{4}{7} = .571429$ and $\frac{3}{5.25} = .571429$.
6. $\frac{6}{2} = \frac{3}{1}$ and $\frac{12}{4} = \frac{3}{1}$ and $\frac{9}{3} = \frac{3}{1}$, so $\Delta KMO \sim \Delta QSU$ by ASA.
7. Much information can be concluded in this figure by thinking about isosceles triangles. However, they are not similar because angles are congruent within triangles, not from one triangle to another. Also, the sides are not in proportion: $\frac{5}{7} = \frac{5}{7} \neq \frac{7}{6}$.
8. Since these are both isosceles triangles with the same vertex angle, their base angles must also be congruent. So they are similar, based on AA~.

Page 42

Often, more than one correct proportion can be used to solve these problems. Only one has been given for each variable.

1.
$$\frac{4}{3} = \frac{x}{1.1} \qquad 4.4 = 3x \qquad x = 1.4\overline{6}$$
$$\frac{4}{7} = \frac{3.2}{y} \qquad 4y = 22.4 \qquad y = 5.6$$

2.
$$\frac{x}{4} = \frac{1}{4.4} \qquad 4.4x = 4 \qquad x = .\overline{90}$$
$$\frac{3.4}{4.4} = \frac{y}{2.8} \qquad 4.4y = 9.52 \qquad y = 2.\overline{163}$$

3.
$$\frac{3.1}{5} = \frac{x}{x+2.1} \qquad 3.1x + 6.51 = 5x \qquad 6.51 = 1.9x \qquad 3.4 \approx x$$
$$\frac{1.9}{5} = \frac{y}{3} \qquad 5.7 = 5y \qquad 1.14 = y$$

4. $\frac{x-10}{x} = \frac{28}{42}$

$\frac{x-10}{x} = \frac{2}{3}$

$3x - 30 = 2x$

$30 = x$

Since $x = 30$, the upper portion of of that side is 20:

$\frac{20}{10} = \frac{51}{y}$

$\frac{2}{1} = \frac{51}{y}$

$51 = 2y$

$25.5 = y$

Pages 43–44 Triangles Exam

1. Vertices: A, D, C Sides: $\overline{AC}$, $\overline{CD}$, $\overline{AD}$

Using a protractor, the measurements of the acute angles are m $\angle ADC$ = 21° and $m\angle ACD$ = 28°. This is an obtuse triangle, therefore, $\angle CDB$ is an obtuse exterior angle.

2. ΔRST is a 30–60–90 triangle, so $ST = 5\sqrt{3}$ and RT = 10.
ΔRUT is a 45–45–90 triangle, so $RU = UT$,

and $RT = RU\sqrt{2}$

$\frac{10}{\sqrt{2}} = \frac{RU\sqrt{2}}{\sqrt{2}}$

$\frac{\sqrt{2}}{\sqrt{2}} \cdot \frac{10}{\sqrt{2}} = RU$

$\frac{10\sqrt{2}}{2} = RU$

$5\sqrt{2} = RU = RT$

The area of RSTU =

$A_{\Delta RUT} = \frac{1}{2}(RU)(UT) = \frac{1}{2}(6.4)(7.7) = 24.64$

$A_{\Delta RST} = \frac{1}{2}(\text{RS})(\text{ST}) = \frac{1}{2}(5)(5\sqrt{3}) = 6.25\sqrt{3}$

$A_{\Delta RSTU} = 24.64 + 6.25\sqrt{3} \approx 35.5$

3. $m\angle HJI$ = 180° – (69° + 67°) = 44°.
$m\angle KJL = m\angle HJI$ = 44°.
$m\angle HJK$ = 180° – $m\angle HJI$ = 180° – 44° = 136°.
$m\angle JKL = m\angle JIH$ = 67° by alternate interior angles.
$m\angle KLJ = m\angle JHI$ = 69° by alternate interior angles.
$m\angle LJI = m\angle KJH$ = 136°.

$HJ = 2.4$

$HJ + JL = HL$

$HJ + JL = 6.7$

$JL = 6.7 - HJ$

$\frac{HJ}{6.7-HJ} = \frac{1.8}{3.2}$

$3.2HJ = 1.8(6.7 - HJ)$

$3.2HJ = 12.06 - 1.8HJ$

$HJ \approx 2.4$

$\frac{1.8}{3.2} = \frac{2.5}{JK}$

$1.8JK = 8$

$JK = 4.\overline{4}$

$JL \approx 4.3$

$JL \approx 6.7 - 2.4$

$JL \approx 4.3$

ΔHJI is not similar to ΔKLJ because the parts have not been named in a corresponding order.
$\Delta HJI \sim \Delta KJL$ because of the AA Similarity Postulate and the SAS Similarity Postulate.

4. $m\angle KML = 90° - 60° = 30°$

$m\angle MDL = 45°$

$m\angle MLD = 45°$

$KM = \frac{4\sqrt{63}}{3} \cdot 2 = \frac{8\sqrt{6}}{3}$

$MD = 4\sqrt{2}$

$A_{\Delta LMD} = \frac{1}{2}\left(4\sqrt{2}\right)\left(4\sqrt{2}\right) = 16$

$A_{\Delta KLM} = \frac{1}{2}(\frac{4\sqrt{6}}{3})(4\sqrt{2}) = \frac{16\sqrt{12}}{6} = \frac{8\sqrt{12}}{3} = \frac{16\sqrt{3}}{3}$

$KL = \frac{4\sqrt{3}}{\sqrt{3}} \cdot \frac{\sqrt{3}}{\sqrt{3}} = \frac{4\sqrt{3}}{\sqrt{3}}$

$LM = \frac{8}{\sqrt{12}} \cdot \frac{\sqrt{2}}{\sqrt{2}} = \frac{8\sqrt{2}}{2} = 4\sqrt{2}$

$KM = \frac{4\sqrt{63}}{3} \cdot 2 = 8\sqrt{}$

$A_{\Delta CMDL} = 16 + \frac{16\sqrt{3}}{3}$ or $\frac{48+16\sqrt{3}}{3}$

$A_{\Delta CMDL} = 16 + \frac{16\sqrt{3}}{3}$ or $\frac{48+16\sqrt{3}}{3}$

These triangles are not similar because their corresponding angles are not congruent.

Perimeter $\Delta KML = \frac{4\sqrt{6}}{3} + 4\sqrt{2} + \frac{8\sqrt{63}}{3} = \frac{4\sqrt{6}+12\sqrt{6}+8\sqrt{6}}{3} = \frac{12\sqrt{2}+12\sqrt{6}}{3} = 4\sqrt{2} + 4\sqrt{6} \approx 15.5$

Perimeter $\Delta MLD = 4\sqrt{2} + 8 + 4\sqrt{2} = 8\sqrt{2} + 8 \approx 19.3$

Perimeter $KLDM = \frac{4\sqrt{6}}{3} + 8 + 4\sqrt{2} + \frac{8\sqrt{6}}{3} = \frac{12\sqrt{6}}{3} + 8 + 4\sqrt{2} = 4\sqrt{2} + 4\sqrt{6} + 8 \approx 23.5$

5. The altitude to the hypotenuse of a right triangle divides the triangle into 2 similar triangles so $\Delta AGB \sim \Delta BGC$.

$\overline{JD}$ is a perpendicular bisector.

$\overline{BG}$ is an altitude.

$\overline{FE}$ is a midsegment.

$\overline{FC}$ is a median.

If $AC = 36$, $FE = \frac{1}{2}(36) = 18$.

6. $\overline{FG} \| \overline{AE}$ because they are both perpendicular to $\overline{DE}$.

Length of $FG = \frac{1}{2}AE = 2.5$.

Length of $HG = \frac{1}{2}BE = 1$.

$FH + HG = FG = 2.5 = FH + 1$, so $FH = 1.5$.

Length of $\overline{DE}$: $A_{\Delta BDE} = 12u^2 = \frac{1}{2}(BE)(DE) = \frac{1}{2}(2u)(DEu)$, so $DE = 12u$.

Area of $ACDB$: $ACDB$ has base $AB = 5 - 2 = 3$ and height $= DE = 12$. So $A_{ACDB} = 3 \cdot 12 = 36$.

7. $A = \frac{1}{2}(9\text{cm})\left(4.5\sqrt{3}\text{cm}\right)$

$= (4.5\text{cm})\left(4.5\sqrt{3}\text{cm}\right)$

$\approx 35.1\text{cm}^2$

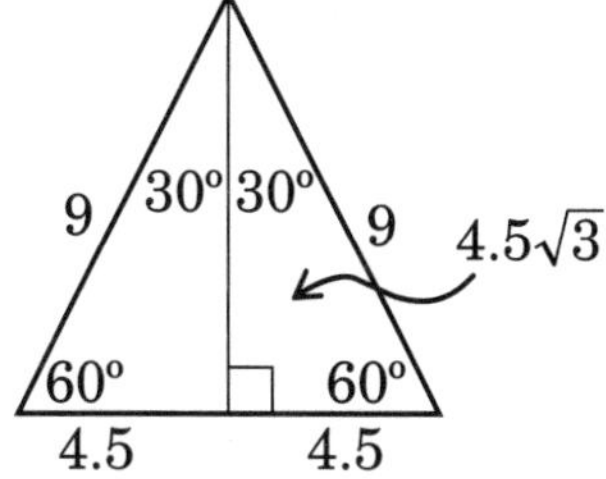

8. Missing measurements: $m\angle IKQ = 180° - 2(34°) = 112°$

$m\angle MKI = m\angle HKQ = 180°) - 112° = 68°$

$m\angle MIK = m\angle HQK = 68° - 34° = 34°$

$m\angle IMK = m\angle QHK = 180° - (68° + 34°) = 78°$

Postulate/theorem: If two angles of one triangle are congruent to two angles of another triangle, then the third angles are congruent. The two triangles share $\overline{QI}$, so they can be proved congruent by the ASA or AAS congruency postulates.

9. Missing angles: $m\angle XNW = 180° - (110° + 39°) = 31° = m\angle AZT$
$m\angle TAZ = m\angle WXN = 110°$
$m\angle ATZ = m\angle XWN = 39°$
Scale factor: $\frac{4}{2} = \frac{2}{1}$
Missing lengths: $\frac{XW}{AT} = \frac{2}{1} = \frac{XW}{1.6}$, so $3.2 = XW$
$\frac{NW}{TZ} = \frac{2}{2} = \frac{6}{TZ}$, so $2TZ = 6$ and $TZ = 3$